Geeking Grifting
and Gambling Through Las V

Fifty Years of Exploits, Ideas, and
Tell All Stories From The Noted Poker Author

By
DAVID SKLANSKY

FIRST EDITION

FIRST PRINTING
Feb 2020

Geeking, Grifting and Gambling Through Las Vegas
Fifty Years of Exploits, Ideas, and
Tell All Stories From The Noted Poker Author

COPYRIGHT © 2020 David Sklansky

For information contact: **David Sklansky**

Table of Contents

Introduction

This book is not an autobiography. I am not famous enough for one and much of my life is not that interesting. But some of it is. More importantly many of the stories that I will be telling you (in approximate chronological order) will not only be interesting (and sometimes juicy tell all stuff) but will often contain a lesson that might be useful to you. Or even to the world in general. Some chapters will not be biographical at all but rather simply explanations of numerous ideas that I have come up with over the years (Some no doubt thought of by others as well,)

Who am I to think that I have dozens of thoughts that are both useful and often unique? It's a fluke. I had a father who was probably one of the smartest men in the world (I'll provide some evidence in the first chapter) who literally gave me a different logic puzzle or high school math lesson virtually every day from age seven to twelve. And I had a father who had a son with three major flaws that made me veer very far from the path he hoped I'd take with my life.

Those flaws were a boredom phobia, a hatred of doing things I didn't want to (eg wearing a tie or studying something uninteresting), and an inability to deal with physical discomfort, especially lack of sleep.

Given the above, it should not be surprising that when I realized that good money could be made from poker and other forms of gambling I made my way to Las Vegas and became the black sheep of the family. (A family otherwise filled with Harvard graduates, authors and professors. See Jack Sklansky, Amy Sklansky, David A. Sklansky, Eddie Miller, Montana Miller, and several others.)

But this unusual history turned me into an unusual man. A high IQ guy who was taught math and logic at a very early age who, as a teenager, stopped thinking about academics but instead thought about scheming my way through the jungles of Las Vegas. The peculiar result, I believe, is a person who has the ability to come up with ideas that can be applied to you and/or the real world. Ideas that I hope will have you saying, "Aha, of course. Why didn't I think of that?"

NOTE: I expect the dates and incidents mentioned will occasionally be slightly inaccurate. However, those inaccuracies will never be of a relevant nature.

Chapter One: Dad

Sometime in 1950, my mother told my father (Irving Sklansky) he had to get a real job. He had a two-year-old son, a chance to make $100 a week working for a union pension fund, and was facing, as far as she was concerned, too much responsibility to accept the (temporarily) lower paying offer to teach math and logic at Harvard. His desire to do the "right thing" and please his wife, caused him to make a decision that he would always regret. Because he was born to teach. In going over his papers after he died, I found much evidence of his talents including, going all the way back to 1938 when he was fourteen years old, where his high school (where he had skipped two grades) wrote "his aptitude in performing and explaining the subject matter (math) is astounding and inspiring."

He went on to get a full academic scholarship to the University of Chicago followed by a full scholarship to graduate school at Columbia University where he got an A+ in every subject. (His math Ph.D. lacked a thesis because of mom.) In between Chicago and Columbia, he was in the Army as were most men his age. But despite World War 2 being in full swing, the Army deemed the best way to use his talent in math and science was to send him to various colleges. Because of that he was subjected to several world class mathematicians and scientists as teachers. Mortimer Adler, famous philosopher who later had his own TV show. Norbert Weiner, inventor of Cybernetics. Arthur Compton, Nobel Prize winner in Chemistry, and Lise Meitner, maybe the greatest female scientist who ever lived. (She didn't get a Nobel Prize but should have as she was the one who got the ball rolling in understanding splitting of the atom.) Plus, several more.

His main professor at Columbia was probably not quite of the intellectual magnitude of those mentioned above but due to one word, he is at least as famous. His name was Edward Kasner. And

5

he realized that we did not have English names for huge numbers that were popping up in math and science. So he asked his young nephew to tell him the name of the biggest number he could think of. The reply was a "googol". Which Kasner used to name the number that is one followed by one hundred zeroes. (He also coined the word "googolplex" which is the unimaginably big number that is one followed by a *googol* zeroes.) That anecdote was fairly well known. But it became a lot better known after a couple of guys decided to name their company after the word he coined (with a slight alteration in spelling.)

Here is part of the letter of recommendation that Professor Kasner sent to Harvard: "Mr. Sklansky has been a student in four of my courses and was sponsored by me for his Master's Degree. He is now working for his Ph,D. Degree at Columbia University and teaching Mathematical Logic at the City College of New York.

He is a mathematician of unusually superior ability and has always done exceptionally fine work in my classes. He is remarkably apt in performing and explaining the subject matter of mathematics, his pedagogy having the same high degree of excellence as his general scholarship. You will find Mr. Sklansky to be resourceful, painstaking, and very industrious. He has consistently done work beyond the scope of his class."

There are many other such letters and anecdotes.

And it wasn't just in math and science that he excelled. For instance, he loved Shakespeare. (And he hated racists.)

So my mom obviously screwed up. Except maybe the fact that he couldn't teach school anymore (he did, part time, later in life) may have been the reason that he spent so much time teaching me when I was very young. And he always made it fun and interesting. In the next chapter I will give you a few examples of the puzzles and lessons he brought up almost every night at the dinner table.

One quick story to show that his talents did not diminish from lack of use even many years later. In 1965 I was studying for the General Mathematics Exam given by the Society of Actuaries. They offered cash prizes for the top five scores in the country for this three hour 70 question test in college math. It was an odd thing to do because the winners were always math majors from the elite colleges. Students who almost never intended to become actuaries. (I passed the test but had no chance for a prize since I took it as a junior in high school.) But even those scholars almost never got a perfect score.

I got ahold of a previous year's test and asked my dad to go over it with me. 15 years after leaving the field, he knocked off each question, one by one, as if he was doing 9th grade Algebra instead of fairly advanced Calculus. Two hours, perfect score.

Finally permit me to quote one last letter in this short chapter honoring my father that has nothing to do with his math ability. This time it comes from Melvin Dykes, who was the head of the pension fund where my father was second in command, on the occasion of Mr. Dykes' retirement:

Dear Irving,

In the hope of creating something different, I discarded the thought of a card. Rather I want to express some personal observations. Simply-among men in all walks of life, I have concluded that you stand head and shoulders above most. This you accomplish in a quiet humble manner, another tribute to your wisdom.

It has been my pleasure and privilege to have you on the team and as a friend.

My best always

Melvin

You will soon see that there were some traits I did not inherit from him.

Chapter Two: Ten Irving Dinner Talks

Before moving on to my exploits and ideas, I thought I would give few examples of the logic puzzles and lessons my father hit me with at the dinner table when I was quite young. (As I got older, they got harder than those below.) You might want to occasionally give one of them to your own kids.

1.   Add up all the numbers from one to 100.

This was the first question my father ever gave me. It really wasn't a question where he expected me to see the trick at age six. Rather he wanted me to know the well-known story about the great mathematician Carl Gauss when he was seven years old and his teacher gave the class this assignment so she could go off shopping or whatever. Problem was that Gauss immediately raised his hand with the answer. Not because he knew the formula for the sum of an arithmetic progression. Rather it was because he immediately realized something. 1+100=101. So does 2+99 and 3+98. In fact, if you add up all the numbers two at a time from the outside in you get fifty 101s. Thus 5050 is the answer.

2.   If three men can build three houses in three days, then four men can build four houses in how many days?

If your kid says "four" it will be a lesson not to jump to conclusions.

3. Ignoring the effect of air resistance if you drop a bullet from 16 feet up, it takes one second to hit the ground. If instead you fire that bullet horizontally (again from 16 feet up) at 1000 miles per hour, it will still hit the ground in one second. My father wanted me to know that at a young age even though Aristotle didn't.

4. George is addicted to unfiltered cigarettes. He smokes 80 percent and then saves the butt so that he can fashion a new one when he has enough butts. If he starts with 25 cigarettes how many does he actually smoke? Of course, the answer is 31.

5. Sally has ten red socks and ten blue socks in her drawer. They are all identical. She goes into her pitch-black room and grabs the minimum number of socks that guarantees she has a pair of the same color. How many socks did she grab? For some reason people often say "eleven" rather than the obvious "three".

6. Three unarmed policemen are escorting three criminals to a remote jail. They come to a river that has a docked boat that can only fit two. The problem is that if the criminals ever outnumber the policeman on either side of the river, they will kill the cops. How do they get across?

    Obviously, you have to start off with one cop and one criminal or two criminals. A criminal remains and the other one returns. The other two criminals now cross and one comes back. (Don't ask me why they don't run away when they are alone on the other side.) So there are three cops and one crook at the starting side. Now two cops cross making it two and two. A cop and a crook come back. The two cops on the original side cross over, get out and the one crook there fetches the other two one at a time. If you are giving this problem to your kid, you should probably make it a bit easier by using two types of coins which he or she can move back and forth across a table.

Interesting anecdote: I happened to give a slightly more complicated version of this problem (only one criminal can operate the boat) to casino owner Bob Stupak, and poker champ Stu Ungar while they were having lunch together. They immediately got six coins and started betting with each other as to who could manipulate the coins properly in the least amount of time. They were at it for almost an hour. I don't think that their obsession with this problem is totally uncorrelated with their success in other areas.

7. Bluefeet always lie. Greenfeet always tell the truth. Three guys with feet covered are sitting next to each other. You ask the first guy what he is. He answers but you can't hear him. The second guy tells you that he said he was a bluefoot. The third guy says "No he didn't. He said he was a greenfoot and in fact he is. What are their true identities? Of course, the key here is that everyone will say that they are a greenfoot. So the second guy lied. And the third guy honestly identified the first guy as a greenfoot.

8. You come to a fork in the road and only one gets you to town. The only person available to give you directions is someone who is one of the aforementioned Bluefeet or Greenfeet. If he is only willing to answer one question how can you query him so that you can be sure of getting to where you are going? There are many similar correct answers. The basic idea is to ask a compound question that will force a liar into a double negative. Something like "If I was here yesterday and had asked you which road led to town, what would you have said?"

11

9.   If the faucet, by itself, fills the bathtub in ten minutes and the shower does it in 15 minutes, how long would it take if they were both on at the same time (and their fill rates remain the same)? This is a routine algebra question. But I didn't know algebra when I was seven. So my father asked me to pretend that the bathtub was 30 gallons. (And if that was not true it was certainly 30 "somethings" as he put it.) So the faucet filled three gallons in a minute and the shower filled two. A total of five gallons per minute. Thus the tub is filled in six minutes.

10.   In a certain small town where beards are forbidden, the lone barber has vowed to shave all the men who don't shave themselves (but never those who do). Who shaves the barber? My father's way of introducing me to Russell paradoxes.

Chapter Three: Troubling Teens

Besides the logic lessons referred to in the previous chapter, my dad also taught me algebra and even basic calculus by the time I was thirteen years old. But there was a downside. Being so far ahead of my classmates, and even sometimes my teachers, screwed me up. It made me abnormal. And not just in a "nerdy" way. It also made me arrogant. For instance, I decided that I would never raise my hand in class to answer a teacher's question unless no one else did. When a substitute teacher gave a true and false quiz that contained one complex curveball, I was the only one who got marked incorrect. When I proved I was right and the teacher changed my score I insisted that all the other scores be changed.

But because I had been taught to be a thinker, I did not easily accept the inevitable path I was leading myself into. Unpopular, arrogant, nerd. On the other hand, there was no way I could will myself to be "normal". And even if I could, I really didn't want to become completely normal since even at this young age it was clear to me that most normal people were unacceptably irrational. So I hit upon a scheme. A not particularly admirable one. Let the most popular kids cheat off me. It worked like a charm. (If it hadn't, my life might have been quite different. Because over the years I have used different variations of this tactic to achieve my goals. Especially in Las Vegas.) Not only were the popular kids (which often included borderline juvenile delinquents, like my future best friend Jackie Stark) happy to get undeserved A's and B's because of me, they also started to appreciate my unusual company.

The one area where this tactic didn't help me was with girls. At least not until I once again used thought to try to remedy the situation. By specifically seeking out detailed advice from those super popular guys who had decided that it was actually kind of cool to be friends with the grifting geek. They got me into the 85 percentile or so.

By the time I was a senior in Teaneck High School in New Jersey, I had no interest in classes and got pretty bad grades. Except in math and standardized tests where I merely had to remember what my father taught me five years earlier. I cut classes, rode a small motorcycle, went to a pool hall almost every day and started to play poker. I routinely was asked over the school intercom to come to the vice principal's office for discipline and I am sure he was mortified that one day he had to both do that and also announce that I was a National Merit Scholarship Finalist (Almost totally based on multiple choice standardized tests.) Likewise, the students in the honors English class were embarrassed that I beat all of them but one on my Verbal SAT. (I wasn't in the honors class.) But in both cases, it was almost solely my 14-year-old brain that achieved those things. Since that time, I was a pretty bad kid.

Some of that was not really my fault. I have some "problems" as I mentioned in the introduction. I can't stand to be bored. Which, among other things means I can't stand trivial chores. Or studying boring subjects. (Which meant that a college degree was almost out of the question.) Also, I have major sleep problems. Not just insomnia. I am far more uncomfortable than most people if I don't have enough sleep. (Which meant that a regular job was almost out of the question.)

So, I found myself at 18 a math prodigy who was great at algebra and probability, who hadn't learned much else, hated school, hated work, couldn't stand waking up before I was ready to, and had had good experiences using my talents to help bad guys do bad things. I passed the first two actuarial exams while still in high school but I hoped against hope that I wouldn't have to do that to survive. I needed to find something that accommodated all my unusual flaws. But what could that be?

14

Chapter Four: College Etc.- My Last Chance For Normalcy

Obviously, my parents were appalled when I started doing poorly in school. My father tried to persuade me that actuaries had very easy, high paying jobs, that I wouldn't mind doing. So I passed the first two of the tests they required and got excellent grades my first semester as a high school senior. That, along with very high SAT scores was just enough to get me into the University of Pennsylvania's business school, otherwise known as Wharton.

But almost immediately I got bored with my classes, started "cutting" them and searched for a poker game. And boy did I found one. Five of the players in that game became great poker players and experts in other games as well. Two were insanely good sports handicappers. One became a "houseplayer" in a major California poker casino. And one (Donald Smolen) wrote the definitive book on Pai Gow poker. Plus me. Undoubtedly a major reason for this was that the players were not really in it for money but rather for the challenge. And because of that, almost every hand was discussed in detail after it was played. When I first started playing in that game, I was pretty good. A year later I was REALLY good. At least at the game they typically dealt, which was seven card hi lo split.

I only lasted a bit over a year at Penn. I got very good grades in the few classes I attended (as did those friends who sat next to me during exams) but could not handle school in general. I did remain friends to this day with the guys I played poker with. One notable anecdote was a trip south that I took with some of them. Part of that trip included a short flight to the Bahamas where I first visited and played at a casino. I had already studied Beat The Dealer and knew how to play and "count" blackjack. But that only gives you a small edge, especially against the four deck shoe they were dealing. I lost $200 the first day. The second day, however, I noticed something. When it came time to shuffle, they were not intermingling the clumps of cards very well. That meant that if I saw a small group of cards contained a large number of aces and tens, I could observe where they were placed and pretty much follow their location in the subsequent shoe.

In other words, it wouldn't be the count that predicted that the next hand *probably* contained better than average cards, but rather the location of sections of cards that *definitely* contained great cards. When those sections were about to be dealt, I significantly raised my bets. And got all my money back plus more. Years later others discovered this trick and named it "shuffle tracking". As far as I know all casinos are now aware of this and shuffle much more thoroughly. But it's always possible that you might find some lazy dealer if you stay on the lookout for one.

I also took a short trip to Las Vegas during my year at Penn and I was pretty much hooked. But I temporarily resisted the urge to move there and instead made one last effort to remain back east and work for a living. Because there was something that was keeping me in New Jersey. Debbie. I had married her and a year later had my son Mathew. And there were two jobs back east that looked like I could maybe tolerate. One of them was a courier. There were many very large corporations that had headquarters on both sides of the Hudson River. And they were willing to pay 100 times the postal rate to get certain letters or packages to the offices on the other side if it could be done in an hour or two. A fellow named Jim Hughes started a company using small station wagons to make these deliveries. And he paid his couriers surprisingly well. The job was pretty easy and there was no boss looking over your shoulder. But the main reason I tolerated it well was that I used gambling theory to take advantage of a kink in the rules!

The station wagons had commercial license plates. Plates that were on trucks but rarely on passenger vehicles. If your vehicle had such plates it allowed you to park for short periods of time in New York City in spots that normal cars could not. However, with those plates you were prohibited from using the highways on either side of Manhattan. Back then it was a $20 ticket if you were caught. Commercial vehicles had to use surface streets. A back and forth trip into downtown Manhattan during weekdays took an extra hour because of that. Couriers who got tickets were responsible for them, whether they were for speeding or whatever. All this set up an obvious risk reward equation for me. Because of one other factor. Cops don't look at the license plates of passenger vehicles when they are on the West Side Highway. I got a ticket exactly once. Which was a small price to pay for getting an hour off in NY to do as I pleased, two or three times a day. (Note: My little scheme did not cost Jim a dime. His net result was virtually identical to what it would be if I followed the rules.)

Of course, this job had no future. So if I was to be a responsible family man with no college degree, it pretty much meant that I start working as an actuary. 99 percent of actuaries graduated good colleges but to become a "Fellow in the Society of Actuaries" you needed only to pass all their tests. Which was my specialty. And since I was one of the extremely small number of students to have passed two tests in high school, Kwasha Lipton, a consulting actuary firm in NJ, took a chance and hired me. I hated it with a passion. Except for one thing. Every actuarial trainee was provided with this newfangled gizmo that had just been invented. A digital calculator. They weren't hand held back then and they were very expensive. But unlike the mechanical ones of the past they gave you the answers instantly (and silently). Meanwhile I was aware that Gardena, California, the poker capital of the world at that time, did not deal the poker game I excelled at (Hi-Lo). The Gardena poker casinos dealt only variations of Draw poker (back then). That game is more mathematical than most and to beat it you need to know lots of different types of odds. Odds that were very time consuming to calculate even for me. Unless of course I had access to an instantaneous calculator.

17

I spent a couple of weeks giving my work assignments short shrift and then quit. Armed of course with almost every fact you could ever need about five card poker. And it was not that much later that I was living in a motel in Gardena.

Chapter Five: First Encounter With Professional Bad Guys

The first year I was out west, I took occasional trips back home. During one of those trips I was invited to a poker game in New York. It was a private game in someone's house and it seemed legitimate. Two of the players were guys in their late twenties who played OK and were also interested in playing craps. There was a craps table there and in that game, they were suckers. They liked betting the "field" of all things, a silly bet with a pretty big disadvantage. I don't remember exactly how I did but I do remember that that they invited me to come to another craps game and bring friends if I liked. Let's call them Izzy and Joe from Brooklyn. Two nice Jewish boys.

They were betting higher than I could afford at the time so I decided to see if I could get some bad Teaneck kids, a couple years older than me, who dabbled in mild criminality to go to the game and give me a free roll. They knew me from their card games and because I was instrumental in seeing to it that they scored well on college entrance exams. Thus, they tended to believe me when I told them that fading field bets was almost a guaranteed win. Still, they replied that it better be and if it wasn't, they would simply take the money. I said "sure fine" not thinking such a thing was likely to happen. The craps game actually occurred in the New York apartment of Johnny, one of the Teaneck toughs. And surprisingly we started out losing. At first, I wasn't worried. But as we continued to lose, I started to think about how this was hurting my reputation with people who did not understand variance.

Johnny excuses himself for a minute then walks returns to the game. With a gun. He robs everyone there (but it's actually only Izzy and Joe's money that he keeps). I am not happy but I have mixed emotions since the guys I touted got their money back. Meanwhile Izzy and Joe seem to forgive me for including a bad apple among those who I invited to the game since I was apparently robbed as well.

Some time passes and I bump into some guys from Penn who occasionally played in the poker game there. More often they bet sports. And they had a lot of money. I told them about these two guys who liked to bet the field and they were interested in fading those bets. I called Izzy and Joe and told them they could play these college kids with no fear that any of them was dangerous. This time the game was at Joe's apartment. With a craps table in the middle of the living room.

While the game is going on, Joe and Izzy ask me a few math questions. Such as "what is the probability that you get exactly five heads if you flip ten coins"? And I had no problem doing that in my head. But I did wonder why they asked.

My friends got destroyed. Something was wrong. Not the dice. Those were ours and they couldn't be counterfeited. Furthermore, it was usually a Penn guy throwing the dice. My friends quit but I was asked to hang back because the two winners wanted to talk to me about something. They told me to sit down. Joe pulls up a chair across from me, takes out a gun and starts pistol whipping my face. About ten whacks. When he stops, he says to me, "We know the whole story. Why, because we are 'connected' (ie associates of one of the New York crime families.) It was a joke that Johnny used his own apartment. Three hours after he robbed us, we and some guys went over there, got back our money, and made him tell us all about you and the plans. So, we know you didn't think we could win but also know you didn't object to a robbery. But we also found out that you are unbelievable with odds. We double checked that with the quizzes we gave you. Because we knew that if you passed them, we wanted you on our side after we smacked you down a little. You are too smart to be on the other side"

Or something along those lines. Then he went to the craps table and rolled ten consecutive double sixes. And Izzy performed a false shuffle that even most magicians, I later found out, did not know about. It turned out that I was in the apartment of two of the best card and dice mechanics who ever lived. And they (supposedly) worked for the Mafia to boot.

I bumped into them on several occasions in Vegas in the ensuing years. Joe made millions at the craps tables there but was eventually barred because he tried to win too fast. Izzy became an excellent honest poker player who even won some tournaments. I never actually did any business with them after that night but remained friendly for obvious reasons. And though I never made a penny with them and would have turned down the opportunity to do so as long as I could do it safely, there is one thing they did do for me. Namely make me realize that the most honest looking people in the world, if they are gambling for high stakes, could still easily be cheaters. Or worse.

Chapter Six: On to Vegas

My life during the early 70s is not worth recounting in this book. I was mainly playing a game (draw poker) that few readers play, so my expertise on that subject probably wouldn't interest them. I had not yet met any politicians, casino owners, or (except for Izzy and Joe) any hardcore criminals or cheats. And I don't think I had yet come up with any great ideas that could change the world.

Then sometime in 1973 I got a call from Crazy Kid with an offer I couldn't refuse. Come to Vegas and he would bankroll my gambling. Everyone called him Crazy Kid because of his nutty demeaner. But he was actually a pretty smart guy, approximately my age. And we had crossed paths several times previously and had several fairly advanced gambling discussions. Apparently, he had gotten ahold of a lot of money and he wanted to stake me in bigger poker games than I had previously played (Gardena casinos had a twenty-dollar limit.) I took him up on it. And promptly got cheated.

"CK" staked me in a 50-100 heads up seven card stud hi lo split game in the Dunes card room. A game that at that time, was never played in Las Vegas. Yet my opponent, a poker pro named Tommy, won the $2000 freezeout in spite of the fact that he frequently made bad plays. Because he often knew my hole cards. He knew them because my hole cards were usually his previous hand's hole cards! There were two cheating dealers at the Dunes who knew how to pull off that move.

How do I know that? Because CK himself told me a few weeks later. And he knew because those same dealers sometimes cheated for him. That's why he had a big bankroll. What had happened is that the people who were behind the widespread poker cheating at the Dunes and elsewhere, decided to recruit this nutty kid to be part of their stable of players who cheated the tourists. They reasoned that no one would suspect him. But CK hadn't realized that Tommy was also part of that stable. (And Tommy didn't realize that CK was.)

Notice I said that the main marks were tourists. The (usually honest) locals were very rarely cheated. It would have been counterproductive to cheat the regulars. Especially if those regulars normally stayed out of the bigger games or games where it was pretty clear that something was going on. Of course, one could point out that the "honest" pros weren't all that honest since they often had an inkling as to what was going on and looked the other way. But to do anything else would have meant a loss of income if not life.

When CK divulged this information to me I asked him to put me in touch with the guy who was setting things up for him. Not because I wanted to become part of the poker cheating group but rather because I had ideas that needed money to implement and because I wanted to know which poker games to avoid. CK complied, perhaps not realizing that after I met "Mark" I would end my deal with him.

The three venues where I sought out a stake horse were blackjack, casino promotions, and (honest) high stakes hi lo split games. We eventually made money together in all three. And in return Mark told me about a lot of nasty stuff. Most of which I will soon tell you.

Chapter Seven: A Blackjack Proposition For "Mark"

When CK introduced me to Mark I had to think of a way to entice him to get him interested in me. I was told that he already was staking poker players, both honest and dishonest, so what did he need me for? My short-term answer was to beat the casinos playing 21. The problem was that this was no longer that easy to do. Beat the Dealer was ten years old by then and most casinos were making it very tough on counters.

But I was way better than most counters. Especially against single decks. And there was a casino that routinely took very big bets, still offered great rules on their single decks and didn't worry about counters as long as they didn't dramatically vary the size of their wagers. And I thought of a deal that would guarantee that I was not trying to simply get lucky with a stake horse's money.

(I was better than the typical counter because I had learned one deck strategy changes that depended on specific cards rather than the count. For example, if there are an excess of sixes left in the deck and you have a 16 vs a ten showing, you would sometimes stand when typical counters would hit. Do you see why?)

The casino was Caesar's Palace. And it was offering a single deck game, dealt down two thirds of the way, where you could double down on any two cards, including after splits, and surrender half your bet on the deal. Plus, they stood on soft 17! Thorp's basic, non-counting strategy, gave the player a small edge against these rules using flat bets. Betting either $100 or $200 and changing your strategy based on cards played was well over a 1 percent edge. And because there were so many high rollers betting $500 chips, $100 bets that would attract attention at other places would fall under the radar at Caesars. A $5000 starting bankroll figured to win at a rate of over $200 an hour with no more than a ten percent chance of being lost.

So my offer to Mark was this: Don't pay me anything out of the first $3000 I win. Since my top bet will be $200 it is unlikely I will reach that threshold if I have no edge. Above $3000 I get half. Mark was only vaguely familiar with blackjack and knew that a lot of supposed counters went broke. So I couldn't persuade him merely by telling him the details of my expertise. But this deal did the trick.

I went on to win about $10,000 before eventually getting barred and pocketed about $3500. More importantly I had started to gain the trust and admiration of someone who had a lot of power in the arena I had chosen for my livelihood. The downside of course was that this fellow, about ten years older than me, was apparently a rather bad man.

Mark was not in the "Mafia". He was Irish which would, I'm told, eliminate him from consideration. But supposedly he was their representative in the professional gambler world back in the seventies. In fact, he told me that himself. I have absolutely no direct evidence that this was true. But no reason to disbelieve it either. (Remember, I had already met two guys, Izzy and Joe who were apparently in the same boat. [Unless of course if their mothers were Jewish and their fathers were Italian. Such a person would both be officially Jewish yet eligible to be "made" I have no idea why my weird mind thinks of those things.]) And there was one anecdote that kind of verifies the claim.

It was about 1978. By then I had made Mark quite a bit of money in both atypical 21 play and a casino promotion. I will describe them shortly. One day I found myself at a Vegas poker room where a gruff looking character came up to me with a disturbing proposition. He knew that I had been making a name for myself as the smart kid in Vegas gambling and he offered to keep me from coming to any harm if I gave him $100 a week. I had previously been told who he was. A bank robber and a murderer who had just spent 20 years in San Quentin and was now making his presence known in Vegas. So, I was inclined to accept his offer even though it was a shakedown. I could

25

afford the $100 and just being seen with him once in a while might actually dissuade someone who thought of robbing me. I was young and not an imposing presence. But before deciding, I asked Mark for advice. I don't remember what he said but I'll never forget what happened a few days later. The murderer sees me and with trepidation comes up to me to offer an abject apology. "I didn't realize who you were". So yeah, perhaps Mark's claims were accurate.

Mark himself was a smart guy and even a very good poker player. In fact, he came up with an ingenious tactic in seven card lowball (Razz) involving a sixth street check that I wrote about years later in Sklansky on Poker. He also told me that he graduated law school. How he found himself in Vegas dictating to professional poker players at the supposed behest of bad guys he never told me. And I never asked.

Chapter 8: Money Falls From The Sky

Before returning to misdeeds and miscreants, lets lighten things up a bit by my telling you of an incident that occurred during this same time period that pretty much assured my prolonged stay in Vegas.

Before I hit Vegas, literally no professional gambler in that town knew how to do basic probability problems. They used flawed estimation techniques or physically dealt out cards or threw dice to come to conclusions with small samples. I was considered a wizard because I could get the exact odds with a pencil and paper and often without them.

One day during the 1974 World Series of Poker, a professional poker player named David Baxter, a man I barely knew, approached me and asked me a lowball draw question. Is a two card draw to A2Joker a favorite over a pat 87654? "Of course not", I said. He replied, "Well Mike C (another pro poker player), wants to deal hands and bet it is". To which I said, "No David, he wants to bet that it is favored over a one card draw to 8765. It's a famous problem because one card draws almost always are better than two card draws but is not in this case. You just heard him wrong".

But Baxter insisted that he heard him right and would I please verify that the pat hand was the favorite. I did the calculation just to be polite. And told him again that the pat hand was a big favorite. David thanked me and walked away.

Twenty minutes later he came up to me and handed me FIVE HUNDRED DOLLARS. That's like a few thousand nowadays. He won two grand and thought it was fair compensation even though I had not taken a piece of the action or expected any kind of freeroll reward. Apparently, Mike C had read about the proposition and misremembered it. And since both he and David were both oblivious to the simplest precepts of probability, I raised my bankroll by a significant amount.

And my optimism as to what lay ahead for me in Las Vegas took a big bump as well.

Chapter Nine: My First Casino (Unwitting) Giveaway

This little exploit occurred shortly after CK invited me back to Vegas. It was a promotion at the Union Plaza hotel involving the Big Wheel. This was normally the worst bet on the casino floor. They spun an upright wheel with 54 slats. Each slat had a picture of US currency and you got paid according to the denomination. So if you bet that the wheel pointer would land on the ten dollar bill, you would be paid ten times your bet if it hit.

The problem was that there were only four spots that showed a ten. So if you made 54 one dollar bets on it, you would average winning forty dollars and losing fifty. A ten dollar loss after betting 54. An 18.5 percent disadvantage. A bet on the one dollar bill had you winning 24 times and losing 30. An 11.1 percent disadvantage.

But the Union Plaza decided to encourage action on this normally dead game by offering one dollar bets at a discount. They were selling a book of twenty coupons for fifteen dollars. And each coupon was exactly equivalent to a dollar bill as long as you used it on the wheel. If you won your bet you not only got paid in cash, you also kept your coupon to play again. But how could this be? A 25 percent discount on bets where the casino edge is less than 20 percent? When I read their ad, I assumed there was a catch. Perhaps a limit of one book per customer. Or maybe a limit of one coupon bet per spin. After all, if you bet a coupon on the ten, you would win ten dollars four times and lose 75 cents 50 times. You would be $2.50 ahead after 54 spins. $50 if you bet the whole book at once. Betting a dollar on the one dollar bill would, after 54 spins have you winning $24 while losing $22.50.

(Note: The ten dollar bet is helped in one respect by the promotion more than the one dollar bet is because it saves 25 cents more often than the one dollar bet saves 25 cents [50 vs 30 per

29

cycle].) On the other hand, the one dollar bet gets to use the coupon more than once much more often which makes up for it.)

But there was no catch. And strangely very few others took advantage of the promotion. They probably assumed that a casino would never offer a bet where they had the worst of it. And like David Baxter and Mike C they didn't bother to try to calculate it out themselves.

I won about a thousand bucks before getting pulled up. In fact, to say that I "won" it isn't really accurate. My edge was too high to have any real chance of losing. It would be closer to the truth to say I was "given" it. So again, I was starting my Vegas adventures off on the right foot. Three nice no risk scores (Caesars, Baxter, Union Plaza) while I was grinding $20 an hour or so in moderately small poker games.

Meanwhile what was the Union Plaza thinking? Their promotion would have every customer winning regardless of their skill. I can think of only one explanation. It has to do with the way casinos evaluate the profitability of their casino games. They don't think in terms of house edge. At least they didn't back then. Rather they thought in terms of "hold percentage". They would count the total amount of money that was used to buy chips at the table and compare that to the amount of money the table actually won. This hold percentage is correlated to the house edge but it is much larger. For instance, a blackjack table typically has a hold percentage of at least 15 percent even though its edge against the average player is about two or three percent. The difference comes from the fact that the chips bought at the table are churned, ie bet several times before they figure to be lost. Someone who buys in with a hundred-dollar bill might bet several hundred dollars before leaving. If he is down twenty bucks when he quits that's 20 percent of his buy in.

The Big Wheel hold percentage is normally well over 50 percent. And some dope at the Union Plaza must have thought that meant he could get away with a 25 percent discount on bets. And no one else bothered to think about it.

Chapter Ten: I'm Warned Off Crooked Poker Games

The $6500 I made Mark from the Caesar's blackjack play was not enough to persuade Mark

to divulge the nefarious goings on in the Vegas poker world. But telling him how to dishonestly beat

the blackjack tables did. Dishonestly but not illegally. I'll go into more detail in the next chapter but

basically the idea was to search out and take advantage of sloppy dealers who sometimes exposed

their hole card. Not only did Mark make a lot of money using this technique he adjusted his opinion

of me from naïve nerd who could grind out a mathematical living, to an ethically challenged fellow

who would be valuable to him. I was essentially back in high school again. (Actually, I considered

taking advantage of casino incompetence less immoral than helping poor students get undeserved

good grades. Both things are called cheating, but given the behavior of casinos, especially back then,

it was only the high school stuff I considered wrong.) Because I was valuable and it didn't seem like

I would be appalled to find out how many poker players cheated, Mark decided that the smart play

was to keep my out of the crooked games.

And if Mark was being honest with me, that was most of them. At least most of the bigger

games at the Dunes and Stardust. The tiny games with monstrous rakes were "honest" and so

apparently were the smaller games at the MGM (now Bally's), the Sahara and the Golden Nugget

(where they were offering a newfangled game called "holdem").

Most of the cheating involved "collusion". Actual card manipulation, marked cards, set up

decks, and the like was not too common (but that would change a few years later). There were some

world class card cheats that would often play in Vegas but ironically when they did, they were

usually the suckers. They got pumped up in out of town games and came back to Vegas where they

played honestly. Honestly but not well. When they cheated they had such a big edge that there was no reason for them to become experts at honest play. (And it would have been dangerous for them to use their cheating techniques in a casino.)

But colluders were different. Non obvious collusion gives you a much smaller edge than cheating with the cards. So you have to know how to play reasonably well. Thus, if you were trying to find a group of players to stake in a colluding ring you were wise to pick them from among those players who were break even or better players. Most non obvious collusion involves saving the occasional bet because a partner has you beaten, or stealing a pot, with the help of a partner, that you wouldn't have stolen if you were playing honestly. I will go into a little more detail in a later chapter. The math of collusive play is actually quite mathematical and interesting.

Not all "teams" were run by Mark. Some, I was told, were controlled by guys who were around before he showed up. Guys with names like "Sarge" and "Shoeshine". But apparently, they didn't get in each other's way. So Mark was able to warn me off their games as well. Meanwhile Mark's competitors got wind of my mathematical abilities and during those early years invited me to dinner a few times. Sarge, Shoeshine, a legendary gambler named Joe Bernstein, and even the Italian fellow who supposedly was behind Mark. And a different Italian fellow who was supposedly the money man for Stu Ungar. Except unlike dinners with Mark, those dinners never included any mention of any activities that they were into. Even though much of it was common knowledge. Rather it was all about picking my brain. Some of the questions could clearly be useful to cheaters and thieves but it was vague enough to give me plausible deniability. Again I was essentially back in high school. And my accurate answers assured me that I would be left alone to make a living without actually getting a job. And, more importantly, I could sleep as late as I needed to.

(NOTE: Although I am not portraying myself that nicely with these anecdotes, I do want to make clear that I absolutely never was even indirectly involved in any serious criminal activity.

Loansharking, prostitution, drugs, robbery, assault and battery or worse. I never heard one word about such things nor was ever asked anything theoretical that applied to such things. The closest to that were the few times when one of those guys explained to someone who was messing with me that he should stop. But I was not told the details of the explanation. Which was fine with me.)

The bottom line was that many of the famous high stakes gamblers sometimes cheated. And that many of the mid stakes poker players often colluded as well. Especially in the Razz games at the Stardust which was a very popular game at the time.

Remember though that the honest pros who had been in Vegas awhile usually knew what was going on. It was actually fairly obvious because the crooked games were usually started by the same group of players and they all stayed in that same game even if there were easier games to change to. Furthermore, those colluders were often friendly with the "honest" players and would warn them off of dishonest games. Not just because they were friends but also because it would be counterproductive to cheat them. There were plenty of tourists. So, some of what Mark told me I would eventually have found out for myself. And like the other ethically challenged "on the square" players, would have looked the other way.

Chapter Eleven: Blackjack Adventures

Almost all professional blackjack players have an extra edge above and beyond merely "counting". They might say otherwise but they do. If you follow the books and find a single deck with good rules you will be playing with a (barely acceptable) one percent edge. But such games are hard to find. Some casinos don't deal enough cards. Some shuffle when you have an advantage but not otherwise. Many restrict doubling down to 10 and eleven and hit soft 17. And of course, most usually deal multiple decks. Each of these things means that flat bets and "basic strategy" have you playing at an initial disadvantage that could be as high as a full percent. Which means that the "count" is rarely high enough to turn things around. The only way to beat such games playing normally, is to bet A LOT more than usual when you do get those good counts (meaning a much larger than normal percentage of aces and tens remain in the deck(s).)

But there are other ways to get an edge that fall short of flat out cheating. One already mentioned is "shuffle tracking". Keeping track of clumps of high cards in a multideck shoe. I don't think this poor shuffling is something you are apt to find nowadays but you never know. Another way is to watch a shoe from the sidelines and jump in only when the multideck has a profitable count. Few casinos still allow that. MIT students did something similar by having a bunch of them betting the minimum at several tables and then signaling their "big player" to come over and bet high because the count was good. Most casinos stopped that by not allowing players to enter the game mid shoe.

But even these techniques were not that appetizing to me and I didn't get involved with them. Too much work for too little gain. Caesar's Palace was a different story because you actually started with a small edge so there was no pressure to play absolutely perfectly. Once Caesar's barred me there was nowhere else to play where mere basic strategy was good enough to win.

Except for the whole darn town of Atlantic City. This chapter ought to be telling you how I won a million dollars during a couple of years of play there. But I was simply too lazy. Too lazy to take advantage of the morons in the New Jersey government who worried so much about exposed hole cards that they instituted a rule that gave basic strategy players more than a half percent edge off the top. And they compounded that error by passing a law that players couldn't be barred unless they were cheating.

The rule that prevented hole card exposure was to not have the dealer get his second card until the players acted on their hands. That was fine. In fact, it meant that double downs and splits were less profitable because, unlike in Vegas, these actions had to be taken before the dealer knew whether he had a blackjack. In Vegas you knew that he didn't have a blackjack when it was time to act. But what more than made up for that disadvantage was that the NJ casinos offered "surrender" where you could forfeit half your bet after getting your first two cards. In Vegas this play was very slightly profitable in a very few circumstances. Because you could only do it against an ace or ten after the dealer checked for blackjack. If she had one you lost the whole bet. But that was not the case in Atlantic City. They offered "early surrender" where you lost only half a bet even if they wound up with a blackjack. Now there were lots of profitable surrender situations especially against an ace. The net result is that many millions were lost to smart players before they changed the rule. Still not sure why I wasn't one of them.

Unless perhaps it was because for a while I was playing with a much bigger edge. Because I sometimes knew the dealer's hole card. There were two basic techniques. One was to find a dealer who didn't protect his downcard well when he checked for blackjack. (Or, if you were willing to commit a crime, a dealer who could be bribed into telling you what he had. Nowadays you can't do this at most casinos as they have a little gizmo that tells the dealer if she has it but doesn't otherwise identify the downcard.) But if you had good eyes, there was a stronger technique. Find dealers who flashed their hole cards as they were sliding it under the upcard. This was called "front loading". There was usually only one seat at the table that would allow you to catch a quick glimpse against these sloppy dealers and that seat could be anywhere, depending on the dealer.

Playing perfect strategy, including buying insurance gave the player about a twelve percent edge. You probably think it would be more and in fact this misconception was later taken advantage of by casino owner Bob Stupak as I will recount shortly. But it was plenty. Of course, there was no way you could actually have anywhere near this advantage since it would require you to make outlandish plays that would give you away. So even if you knew the hole card every time your real edge was more like 5 percent. Since you would sometimes miss seeing it, 3 percent was probably the real-life number. But that was still plenty. And a few dozen people were making a lot of money doing this. It was not as profitable for me because I had become known as a counter and was subject to extra scrutiny. To ameliorate that I taught my girlfriend Sherry and brought out from New Jersey my buddy Jackie Stark to help me. We even went to Reno to play. Eventually we all got barred even though they couldn't figure out what we were doing. At that point I told Mark about the technique. And, as I mentioned earlier, he reciprocated by making sure that I knew about any nasty goings on that could possibly affect me.

NOTE: In case you are wondering, front loading was deemed legal by the Nevada Supreme Court. As long as you weren't aided by a device like a prism or a wheelchair you didn't actually need. They hated to rule against casinos but they were worried that a tourist would accidently notice the flashing dealer, take advantage of it, and get arrested.

Meanwhile their decision caused the downfall of a well-known casino. (I won't name them because my knowledge is second hand.) This casino, among others, supposedly dealt with cheaters by beating them up rather than arresting them. And they always got away with it because, to the cheaters, that was the lesser of two punishments. Then one day they administered the beating to two young guys who were catching hole cards. Because they didn't know it had been ruled legal. Normally that would not have been a fatal error. Both because the miscreants knew they were in the wrong, morally if not legally, and because the owners of the casino were feared throughout Nevada. The problem was that these kids were from New York and both their fathers were attorneys. New York attorneys like big lawsuits more than they fear cowboys or worry about immorality. And that casino was practically put out of business and never was the same after that. Or so I was told.

Chapter Twelve: Not Hi Lo - HOLDEM!

Almost all larger poker games in Vegas casinos in the mid 70's were either seven card stud

high or seven card stud low (Razz). There were a very few draw games, occasionally a big no limit

deuce to seven game, and Binion's Horseshoe had begun to stage an event they called the World

Series of Poker that used No Limit HoldEm for their main tournament. And the Golden Nugget had

started to spread 10-20 limit holdem. But I had never played holdem. And Razz games were

simplistic and usually dishonest. So I stuck to stud. And then hi lo came to town. The seven card stud

variety. Yum. This was the main game that me and my buddies played and analyzed at Penn. None

of the Vegas players, save a couple of pros from New York, knew how to play it. The Sahara was

spreading a 15-30 every night so that became my regular hangout for a while.

The 1975 World Series of Poker had a hi lo tournament. I came second to Doyle Brunson.

For those who know a little bit about regular hi lo stud (not "eight or better") you might be interested

to know that the final hand had me and Doyle putting in about ten bets each on fourth street. He

showed 82 offsuit and I showed 86. I turned over a 54 and he turned over A2. He had the better high

hand and the better low draw and couldn't understand how I could put in so many bets. The answer

of course was that in spite of his lead in both directions I had the slightly better hand. All that matters

is who would "scoop" more often and I knew that was me.

People pretty much realized I was the best hi lo player in town, at least in full games (since

they are more mathematical in nature). And this resulted in a business proposition to me. It was made

by John Luckman the owner of a famous establishment in Vegas called the Gamblers Book Store. It

carried about a thousand titles, every one gambling related. In 1976 John hatched a plan to publish a

couple of dozen 64-page booklets about all sorts of gambling games, sell them for two dollars each, put all of them on a metal rack, and get that rack into the gift shops in the casinos. He got in contact with me and asked me if I would write the book(let) on hi lo. I would get ten cents for every one sold. Ten percent of the wholesale price. It was a nice compliment, but it didn't really appeal to me for various reasons. The main one being that there were already a few books that had decent chapters on the game.

But the same was not true for holdem. If I wrote a book about that game it would be the first one. And it looked like holdem was the up and coming game. Texans had been playing it for several years and it was starting to spread. The attraction seemed to be that there were no folded upcards to memorize as there was in stud. The only problem was that I had only played the game a handful of times. But I wasn't worried. I knew that I could play it a few more times while thinking about what I would write, and come up with a better book than most Vegas pros who had played it for years. I made my counter offer to John and he accepted. He quickly sold about 30,000 copies for $2.00 and then $2.95. When he died the book wound up with my publishing partner Mason Malmuth, (whom I will have more to say about later), who now sells it for twenty bucks. Total sales are now about a quarter of a million.

(Interesting anecdote: The first printing of 3000 copies had a major flaw on the cover. The words of the title were yellow and very hard to read because the background was yellow as well. That was fixed in the second printing of 5000. The third much larger printing was fine and the price was hiked to $2.95 [John could have easily gotten $5 at that point but he kept it cheap as a way to imply that this now famous book was in a similar category to the group of booklets on the rack.]

As years went by most of my readers had bought the later sturdier editions. Those printed by Gambler's Book Store were rather flimsy and didn't stand the test of time. Even I had no copy of the first printing. That bothered me because I realized that for several reasons it could be quite valuable.

The book was well known and it was still selling many copies 40 years later. Since it was flimsy there were probably very few. if any. in existence and most of those would be in poor condition. And the first edition was instantly identifiable and unique because of the cover flaw. Occasionally a poker player would come up to me and tell me that he still had an original book. But when I asked them to show it to me it was almost always the $2.95 third printing. Rarely was it the second printing. And it was never the first. Then one day around 1995 I got a call from the new owners of the Gambler's Book Club telling me that they had an original. I went over to see it. It was in quite bad shape with lots of writing inside. I wasn't too enthused with owning it. On the other hand, it was starting to look like this was the only copy in existence.

For some reason I recounted this story to my father on one of my phone calls back home. I don't remember his reply. But it gave no inkling of what was to come next. A package arrived a few days later and in it were three UNOPENED MINT copies of that first edition. He had saved them all those years. I still haven't decided what to do with them. But if I do sell one it won't be cheap.)

By the way for those of you who are worried about all those poker players from whom I withheld my wisdom about hi lo split, you will be glad to know that when Doyle Brunson decided the next year to write his epic poker book Super System, he chose me to write his Hi Lo section. Check it out. That book is also still in print.

Chapter Thirteen: Another Book And A Lesson

When I saw how well Holdem Poker was received, I started to consider pivoting away from gambling, at least a little bit, and explore writing a little more. Although I'm a mediocre writer I considered myself a good explainer. When I tutored math, my students usually got A's or raised their SAT scores by at least 100 points. And it looked like I was able to transfer that to the written word. Of course, part of my first book's success resulted from it being the only one to address a new popular game in detail. And another part involved the unique nature of holdem which made it unclear whether one starting hand was better than another one. I came up with a chart that (approximately) ranked starting hands from best (AA) to worst (27 offsuit) while putting them into eight groups. It was this chart that made the biggest splash and a slightly amended version is still referenced today.

But there were other concepts in that book that had never really been written about previously. "Semi-bluffs", "Implied Odds", "Effective Odds", "Inducing Bluffs" and a few others. Those were the names I coined for them in that book and they are still in use today (usually without giving me credit.) But those concepts were not fully explored for poker in general, as the book was about one game only. Plus, there were many other general concepts rolling around in my head that weren't in that first book.

So, I asked John Luckman whether he would be interested in publishing a more general poker book. One that differed from all others because it wouldn't be a "how to" book but rather one that focused on the theoretical concepts that underlie good poker strategy. He readily agreed. Except this time, I wanted to tape record the contents rather than write it out longhand as I did with Holdem Poker. He agreed to that as well. The result was "Sklansky On Poker Theory". The book had very good information but because of how it was produced it did not make for easy reading. In spite of

that, serious poker players bought it at a pretty good clip.

Then one day a poker player who knew people at the major publisher, Prentice Hall, told me

he would be willing to put me in touch with the company to have them take it over. I said that would

be great. They told me that if they published the book, they would change the title to Winning Poker

so as not to scare off readers with the word "theory" (My suggestion was to rename it "The Theory of

Poker") and I reluctantly agreed. I also agreed to rewrite it and make it more accessible to beginners.

But before they made a decision, they wanted to run it by an editor to get his input. His name was

David Heineman.

What I am about to tell you next is something I had previously described in my book DUCY.

And it got some pushback from readers who thought that my actions were wrong. I still vigorously

disagree. Let's see what you think.

After two weeks with no reply I called the editor to see if he had come to a decision. He told

me that he was rejecting the book. He thought it was good but wasn't the type of book Prentice Hall

was looking for. Because of the way my mind works I immediately saw a connection to pit bosses in

casinos who sometimes barred "tough" craps players even though the house had an advantage over

them. These guys would walk in with $100 and either blow it or (very rarely) leave with $5000.

From the pit boss's perspective this player could cause him problems with *his* bosses (unless they

fully understood gambling concepts) those few times the player made a score, but he would never get

any credit when the player lost a hundred. So, the pit boss would back the guy off.

I perceived this editor to be thinking along the same lines. He didn't know much about poker

except that a book about niche subjects would never become a blockbuster. The best he could hope

for would be a moderate success. For which he would get little credit. But in his mind, it could be a dud which would be a mark against him if he recommended it be published. So, I had to figure out how to change his personal risk vs reward equation. I replied to him "Perhaps you don't know that the original book has already sold well in the poker community and is getting great reviews. A slightly simpler version published by a major publisher will almost certainly do even better. I am getting pretty well known due to my first work and success as a gambler and I think that there is a very good chance that after I find a major publisher to print it, I will be doing a lot of interviews. And when I am asked something like 'what made you switch from Gambler's Book Club to Simon and Schuster', I will always reply, 'well actually I first went to Prentice Hall. But an editor named David Heineman turned me down.' There was a three second pause. Followed by the reply "let me reconsider". Those were his exact words. I had changed his personal upside vs downside calculations so that they would coincide with the truth. If that took some nastiness on my part, so be it.

The book did well for Prentice Hall but not nearly as well as it did after Mason and Two Plus Two Publishing took it over and changed the name to *The Theory of Poker* as it should have been all along. It is now, to my knowledge, the best selling poker book of all time (Doyle's Super System I believe is close). It has sold a half a million copies or so and in spite of mainly targeting limit rather than no limit poker (My new book *The Theory of Poker Applied To No Limit* takes up the slack) is still going strong (often still #1 rated among poker books on Amazon.)

Chapter Fourteen: Two Good Horse Racing Situations

Among the various casino errors or promotions that I spotted and took advantage of in my early years in Las Vegas were two that involved horse race betting. I consider them both interesting and instructive which means that they need to be included in this book.

The Bingo Palace (now the Palace Station) was holding a horse race handicapping contest somewhere in the same time frame of my first two books being written. I thought that it would be a nice break from writing if I could find an edge. It couldn't come from handicapping expertise because I was only good rather than great at that endeavor. But tournament theory was another story. Whether it be poker, blackjack, craps or horseracing, the best players were often underdogs to tournament specialists because the rules of the tournament were often such that the normally correct play became wrong. That was clearly the case in this horse race tourney, at least to me and a few others.

Every entrant was given $100 in play money each week for four weeks. The entrants were allowed to spread win, place, or show bets of $20 any way they wanted to. Including not making all five bets. The player who moved his $400 to the greatest play money figure won the $10,000 prize. In other words, the entrants, of which there were a few hundred, were told to make up to 20 $20 bets and get a final result that beat everyone else.

All good handicappers know that on average, the higher the odds a horse is, the worse a bet it is. On average, win bets have about a 20 percent disadvantage. But random bets on favorites lose less than 10 percent while random bets on big underdogs lose about 50 percent. In other words, a 100-1 shot wins only about once in 200. They are virtually always sucker bets. But not in this tournament. In fact, any bet other than win bets on giant underdogs was, until you hit one, idiotic. Think about it.

Any player who restricted his twenty $20 bets to horses that figure to pay about 100 to 1 had about a ten percent chance to hit one. If he did, his play bankroll would be about $2000. Since some players would be making these types of bets, it was almost certain that someone would wind up with well over $1000 by tournament's end.

Given that, it becomes obviously ridiculous to bet on horses 5-1 or lower. You would have to win almost all of them to outperform someone who hit even one very big longshot. That's almost impossible But it would also be wrong to try to hit two *semi* big longshots. If you stuck to 40-1 shots you were very unlikely to win the contest with one winner and two winners would be iffy. Yet two 40-1 shots out of twenty tries is a lot harder than one 100-1 shot. The bottom line is that the vast majority of entrants who paid $25 each were throwing their money away on stupid bets.

I got lucky the third week and hit a 120-1 shot. Nothing that big had come in previously. I was well in the lead. Except somebody else had been following a similar strategy and hit the same horse. We were tied. Had I known who it was I might have suggested to him that neither one of us bet anything the last week. Thus, almost certainly guaranteeing us five grand each. But I didn't know who it was. So now it became interesting. I had to guess what he would do (given he almost certainly knew he was tied with someone.) I thought his most likely play was to not bet at all hoping either that I would do the same or perhaps even make bets favored to lose. If he didn't bet, my play was obvious. Do you see it? Think for a minute. It would be to find a monster favorite and bet on it to show. That would make me over 90 percent to win rather than lose, an extra 5K. The problem was that he might deduce that I would do that. Which would give him the counter strategy of making a slightly riskier (but still probably "show") bet that was still well over 50 percent to hit that would pay a bit more than my show bet would pay. And if I was sure he would do that, my play would now be to make a bet that was only 60 percent or so to win that figured to pay more than his winning bet.

46

But because we were anonymous to each other I went with the first option of betting $100 on a big favorite to show. That's the right play if he bets nothing, or bets a smaller amount to show on a big favorite or if he is silly enough to make a risky bet in that last week. I don't know how he played it but I do know that my show bet hit, paid $2.10, and I scooped the 10K. Probably because I won the tournament by five dollars.

The other edge I found in horse race betting involved something called "house quinellas". This was a bet that did NOT get mingled in with the racetrack pool. In other words, it was not pari-mutual. The race books kept the action to themselves because it was quite profitable. Except in one case.

A quinella is like an exacta except the order doesn't matter. Just pick the first two horses. The house quinella payoff was figured by multiplying the win price of the winner by half the place price of the second horse. This was not usually a fair payoff. But if the two best horses in the race were about equal and the other horses had almost no chance, you had an anomaly. The fair price for the quinella would now be SMALLER than the fair price of the winner (which could never happen with house quinella payoffs). Think Affirmed and Alydar. It was easily 80 to 90 percent that they would come in one-two but it was a tossup who would win. The mutual would be something like like $3.80 to win and $2.20 to place either way. Probability wise, the quinella should be no more than $2.80 but the house quinella comes out to at least $4.00. Of course, situations this extreme were very rare. But they didn't have to be this extreme to give you an edge. Two horses below 3-2 were probably good enough. Just another way to grab some money from people who weren't as smart as they thought they were.

Chapter Fifteen: Developing Thoughts. Starting With Crime And Punishment

This will be the first of a few chapters where I tell you about ideas that have popped into my head in the last 40 years that are not directly about gambling. Some I have written about previously. Some have undoubtedly been thought of by others even though I am not usually aware of them. Some may seem controversial at first glance but I think that in most cases I can persuade you that they really are not. Hopefully you will agree with me, perhaps even say to yourself, "Aha. Why didn't I think of that?"

Several of the ideas that started entering my head after I had written a few books involved crime and punishment. This should not be surprising because the ideas involved similar thought processes to those used in poker. This chapter will mention four of them.

1.   Probably Guilty Verdicts

2.   Positive EV Crimes

3.   Unreasonable Doubt and the Death Penalty

4.   Eliminating Murder Freerolls.

Notice that all four of these subjects were described with words that are also used in gambling.

Before describing each of these ideas in more detail let me make clear that I am fully aware that it is a lot easier to advocate the logical theory behind them than to implement them in practice. However, I think that if people see that the logic is undeniable, they will go to the trouble to iron out the details.

A. Because it is considered so important that we don't convict innocent people it is inevitable that we acquit a lot of guilty ones. There is no way around it. Judges don't usually spell out a specific probability percentage that a juror needs to convict someone, but it's almost certainly at least 90 percent in order to be labelled "beyond reasonable doubt". While most people who are arrested are easily over 90 percent to have done it, those clearcut cases are usually plea bargained. The ones that go to trial are often not slam dunk convictions. But the acquittals are often only because the 90 percent certainty has not been reached. It's not because the jurors think the defendant is probably innocent. In other words, a pretty high percentage of acquitted defendants are actually guilty and the jurors know it. They voted to acquit someone who they would not bet was innocent.

In most cases this is an unfortunate fact that we have to live with. An acquitted defendant gets to live exactly as if he was deemed completely innocent even if the jurors had serious doubts. And I think that for some very serious crimes that should change. Child molesting being perhaps the most obvious example. For such crimes the jurors should be allowed to render a verdict of "probably guilty" and law enforcement and others should be allowed to behave toward defendants who got such verdicts differently than those who received not guilty verdicts.

B.   The punishment is supposed to be correlated to the seriousness of that crime. But there is a problem with that, especially regarding crimes that simply steal money. Some are so unlikely to result in the perpetrator being caught, that a criminal who is trying to decide whether to commit that crime can use the same technique as a poker player who is deciding whether to make a very large bluff. After which he may realize that the small chance of being caught is worth accepting, given the reward. If the punishment is a fine, it's a straight up gambling problem. And if its prison it is still essentially a gambling problem if the criminal assigns a dollar amount to what he would need to be paid to do the time. And if those calculations come out to a positive expected value, then the punishment is not a sufficient deterrence. I maintain that it needs to be greater even if that violates the proportionality concept for punishments.

        Of course, one problem that arises with my idea that punishments should be increased for crimes that have a low probability of being prosecuted is, "how do you determine that probability?". Maybe so. But nowadays there are clearly some financial crimes that are so easy to get away with that they are undebatably "good plays" given the punishment for them. For instance, the telephone scams that usually target the elderly. I say that if these people are caught and convicted, put em in jail and throw away the key.

C.   It is reasonable that the "beyond reasonable doubt" criteria does not mean that a juror be 99 percent certain that a defendant is guilty before convicting him. Otherwise we could rarely convict anyone and people would not be safe. The few innocents that will be convicted using our present criteria is a price that we have to pay for that safety. Plus, if they are ever exonerated they are almost always instant multimillionaires which takes the sting out a bit.

(There will also be a chapter near the end of this book that will hopefully reduce the unjustly incarcerated even further.)

But there is no reason that a 99 percent (or higher) threshold should not be used to keep someone from being executed. Not if he will definitely be doing life without a chance for parole if he is spared. If you are going to insist on having the death penalty then a "shadow of a doubt" of his guilt should be a mitigating circumstance that stops the execution. Morally that is a slam dunk is it not? I do see one problem with this idea. The general public does not want to admit to themselves that innocent people might be getting convicted. And if my idea is implemented it would mean that we are admitting that some who are serving life sentences, but were spared because of shadow of a doubt, could have as much as a 3 or 4 percent chance of being innocent. That will bother some people. But it's not a good enough reason to reject my idea.

D.	As much as we are disgusted by rewarding a hostage taker, a kidnapper, or an escaped convict (including those who have already killed) in return for not killing again, I say we have no choice. We can't be giving these people "freerolls" where they have nothing to lose when they murder someone. I won't bother to give specific examples as I think they are pretty obvious.

Chapter Sixteen: Barred And Bored

My Vegas blackjack career essentially ended around 1980. Casinos, with the help of a detective agency, shared information as to whom to back off from the 21 tables. So it was back to grinding poker. Usually 15-30 hi lo, and 10-20 Hold em. The royalties from my first two books didn't amount to very much at first so I had to put the hours in if I wanted to maintain the nice lifestyle I had with Sherry, plus pay child support, plus fly back to NJ every few weeks to see my son.

One day I am playing holdem at the Nugget and I spot a private detective who knew me. I made the mistake of approaching him to tell him that I had no intention of playing anything other than poker. In fact I sometimes even played with Nugget owner Steve Wynn who had read my book and occasionally talked to me about it. But instead of giving me a pass, the detective went to the casino manager who promptly barred me from the whole casino. I was pretty sure I could get the decision reversed and the opportunity presented itself shortly thereafter. There was a wealthy hi roller from New York named Jerry Jacobs who not only gambled high at the Nugget but also was, a personal friend of Mr. Wynn. I gave Jacobs several lessons plus won him some money when he staked me in a game. I asked him to intervene in my situation and he agreed to talk to Steve about me.

Steve called me on the phone to tell me that he turned Jerry down. That's obviously very unusual since guys that are barred from casinos are rarely worthy of a call from the owner. But it happened because Steve actually didn't actually want me barred. His problem was that he didn't want to embarrass his casino manager by overruling him. That had to be his priority. However he wanted me to understand and essentially called me to apologize. He suggested that I find a way to convince the casino manager that I should be unbarred which I was eventually able to do a few years later. But for the time being, I had to deal with the fact that one of the main places I had been playing at was no longer available.

(Notice that this is similar to the Prentice Hall situation. It is not enough to have an idea, request, or criticism that the top guy will be glad to hear. If someone under him has a problem with what you have to say, you could easily be rebuffed by the top guy so as not to ruffle feathers.. The above incident was actually repeated with me a few times. For instance, when I told Bobby Baldwin about some silly errors the Bellagio sports book was making, he declined to fix them because it would have embarrassed his sports book manager who was generally doing a good job.)

With one major Vegas casino gone, three reasons to move to Reno started to loom large. A major casino hotel (MGM, now Grand Sierra) with a poker room had just been built. There was still a possibility of getting in some blackjack play in Reno's casinos, and most importantly, I had just made a deal with my ex-wife Debbie where I paid her way to move out west with Matty and her husband. They accepted. We all thought she would wound up somewhere near the Pacific Ocean. But instead they fell in love with Truckee, 30 miles west of Reno. So Sherry and I packed up and headed north.

We didn't stay that long as other opportunities arose. But before we went back to Vegas something happened in the MGM poker room that was to portend the future for me. I was playing 15-30 holdem when I was tapped on the shoulder by the poker room shift boss who told me that the casino manager was standing at the cardroom entrance and wanted to talk to me. Uh oh. Who recognized me? I went up to him pondering how to assure him I would stay away from the pit if he would allow me to continue to play poker. His words to me were "I heard you were here playing poker. And I just wanted to say that I read your book and wanted to tell you how much I enjoyed it."

I had reached a bend in the road.

Chapter Seventeen: Math Ignorance Creates My No Risk "Score"

I'm back in Vegas now and as usual I'm reading the paper with my afternoon breakfast. I come across an ad for the new more liberal football parlay card the Stardust was offering. Parlay cards used to be complete sucker bets that were mainly targeted to one dollar bettors. Bet five games, and get at most 20-1 on a 31-1 shot. An eight teamer payed about 70-1 instead of the true odds of 255-1. The true odds on a ten teamer are 1023-1 and the original cards payed only 100 for1. But they softened that a little by also giving you 10 for 1 for nine out of ten. Still only a return of about twenty cents on the dollar.

But somewhere around 1980, Vegas sportsbooks realized that they could get much bigger parlay card bets if they made the odds more reasonable. And in the previous few weeks there was a sort of parlay card war among the sportsbooks that had reached the point where they were paying back about 70 percent. The ten teamer was paying 160 for 1 plus 60 for 1 if you hit nine out of ten. You figure to hit nine out of ten, ten times as often as ten out of ten. Your payback would thus theoretically be 760 out of 1024. (Actually, astute players did a bit better than that because the cards were printed early in the week with fixed pointspreads. Sometimes those pointspreads moved by gametime so parlay card bettors who waited until game day could pick teams that were getting one or two points more on the card than the final line would give them.)

Knowing about the parlay card war, I barely glanced at the ad. No way this week's payback could come close to the 100 percent I would need to consider it. Or so I thought. And I almost missed the play that increased my bankroll, percentagewise, by more than any other play in my career. Because not only did the Stardust's cards pay back 100 percent it paid back over 160 percent! I couldn't believe my eyes. The ad showed a picture of the card. A card whose ten game parlay not only paid 160 for 1 for ten wins and 60 for 1 for nine wins but also 20 for 1 for eight wins. Could they really be this dumb? Educated ninth graders know that there are 45 ways of picking eight out of ten. If you bet every combination for a dollar each you would get back 160 + 600 +900 dollars no matter what happened (except sometimes if you bet non half point lines on "ties lose" cards). The cards had a $100 limit. So if you handed the Stardust 1024 cards and $102,400 they would soon owe you $169,840. Assuming they would pay.

But I wasn't so sure they would. In fact I was pretty sure they would wake up to their error well before the games began. Plus, I didn't have that much cash. So I turned to Mark. He was neither worried about their paying or surprised by their stupidity. In fact, he later told me that he found a private bookie to take the same bets. A guy who obviously couldn't do simple math and must have assumed that if the Stardust was booking it, the math must be fine.

Now the above description is somewhat simplified. Only seven of the games had half point lines that couldn't tie. So I had to come up with a scheme that required hedge bets and offered up the possibility of "middles". It was really quite ingenious if I do say so myself. But I don't want to get into the weeds here. Except to say that the scheme impressed Mike as much as finding the math error did. The bottom line though was that by using my instructions it was a riskless way to duplicate (plus more) the results of the simplistic strategy of betting every combination. Mark put up all the money. And there were no surprises with the results. But would Mike pay me my end? On Monday he came to our apartment and handed me over THIRTY THOUSAND DOLLARS. For taking no risk and doing a math problem my father taught me when I was nine.

Even though Mark put up the money and did most of the work, in no way did he begrudge me the payoff (Remember he himself made ninety grand.) In fact, it was quite the opposite. I was an asset he was not about to risk losing. Which meant among other things that when I was playing poker (or sometimes backgammon) with my own money, I would never be in one of those games that was not "on the square". If that meant I was to learn the names of all the cheaters, including some surprising ones, so be it.

Chapter Eighteen: When Good Players Collude

Eric Drache, one of those higher stakes players that Mark said was actually honest, was having a bad run in his usual game of 30- 60 seven card stud, high only. And he was lamenting to me how whenever he had the low card that was forced to bet ten dollars into the starting pot containing five dollar antes, late position steal raisers (to $30) always seemed to have the goods. He was calling and reraising many of those raises under the assumption that they were often weak and was losing a lot because they somehow usually weren't. The explanation of course was that colluding players were signaling the strength of their hand to each other and allowing it to get to the steal position only if that partner had a good hand. And this one tactic was more than enough to insure that the colluders had an edge, especially if the ante was large and the "marks" were tough players who aggressively defended their bring ins. Eric really should have figured this out for himself but he was probably blinded a little by the fact that the guys who were cheating him, he thought were his friends. Plus, the fact that he knew they played well enough to win without cheating. I probably could have figured out that the game was dishonest both because of the ante steal anomaly and because some players had pushed for extra big antes, (presumably, but not actually, to thwart weak but tight players.) But I didn't have to figure it out because I was told about them.

Note: I should probably mention right now that the reason I was never asked to be a member of these teams was not because I was deemed too honest too participate. Rather it was because I had the reputation for avoiding close gambles and tougher games. It would have looked odd if I was playing at a tough table as colluders often do. I think I would have declined an offer to participate but who knows?

There is a chance that my knowledge that very good players sometimes cheated may have actually hurt me. I had thought rather deeply about the "theory of collusion" and realized that a few colluders who played a decent honest game, need not do anything obvious to have enough of an edge to be more of a favorite than the world's best player playing on the square. Especially if they formed large teams which would allow them lots of different combinations of three or four partners. Which was of course exactly what team builders like Mark were doing. This prevented honest players from getting suspicious if they saw the same players were always playing together. (Playing on the internet would require one extra tactic. Since the sites can track your results and big winners would be scrutinized, it would be necessary to add partners who were not colluding, that you could sluff off most of your winnings to.) Since I knew the strength of colluding, knew how easy it was to gain an edge without getting caught, and because of Mark's revelations, knew that there were plenty of players who were, besides skillful, willing to add those edges, I stayed away from tough games. I also stayed away from slightly advantageous plays that required big money and big money games in general. I felt I needed a cushion in case I was sometimes against players with extra edges. But that prevented me from entering the upper echelons of high stakes play. I'll never know for sure if that paranoia helped or hurt me in the long run.

Chapter Nineteen: Mafia Front Man's Surprising Reply

Here's a short anecdote to perhaps break up the tales of Vegas seediness back in the day.

It was common knowledge that the hidden owner of the Dunes in the seventies was the mob. Which was probably why their cardroom was chosen to deal the crooked games. But just as in the other Vegas casinos that were purportedly owned by the mob, the Dunes had a front man that was technically the owner. (I know none of this first hand, but it was considered common knowledge.) In the case of the Dunes that owner was Sid Wyman, a well-known character in Las Vegas at the time.

Meanwhile there was an investigative reporter for The Arizona Republic newspaper named Don Bolles who was writing articles exposing mob activities. In 1976 he was murdered with a car bomb. Of course everyone assumed it was a mob hit even though they normally didn't kill reporters. It was big news. The day he died I happened to be in a sportsbook where Sid Wyman was reading the form. I barely knew him but for some reason I thought it would be interesting to see how he would reply if I asked him what he thought of the Bolles murder, given his supposed ties to the organization allegedly responsible for it. Plus, the general dislike for "snitches" in that neck of the woods. Would he say something like "it served him right"? Nope. His reply was "That man will live forever". You never know.

Chapter Twenty: My Stupak Saga Begins

Bob Stupak was a very unique character. He never got past eighth grade. But when he died, he left as part of his legacy the most iconic tower in the United States, a Las Vegas street named after him, and a reputation for out of the box, sometimes wild, and sometimes ethically dubious schemes. And I was a part of much of that.

Remember that this book is not an autobiography. I'm giving short shrift to purely personal details of my life and concentrate on things that contain a lesson that might be useful to the reader. But that includes almost all my adventures with Bob (some of which were first recounted in my book DUCY.)

I first met Bob at the World Series of Poker at Binion' Horseshoe in the late 70's. He had just built his small hotel casino called Vegas World on a seedy section of Las Vegas Boulevard between the strip and downtown. He barely knew the rules of poker but he was always looking for publicity and the WSOP in April was where the media hung out back then. When he showed up, I thought this might be my chance to get involved with a sole owner who I could really help with my gambling expertise. When I introduced myself to him, he didn't know who I was. So, I told him that I knew more about gambling than anyone else in the world. To which he replied, "then tell me the house edge on Crapless Craps". Not the reply I expected but one that was quite fortuitous for me. Because it was exactly the type of question that almost no gambler or casino employee knew how to do, but was a piece of cake for me.

The basic rules of regular craps has you throwing two dice, winning your bet immediately if you roll seven or eleven, losing immediately if you throw "craps" which is two, three, or twelve and establishing a "point" if you throw 4,5,6,8,9,or 10. If you establish a point you keep throwing until you roll it again, (which is a winner), or a seven which would mean you lost. Crapless Craps, as Bob called it, was a game someone recommended to him, that considered all numbers except seven as a point. Regular craps has a house edge of 1.4 percent. You average losing $1.40 for every hundred dollars you bet. Crapless Craps turns three automatic losers into possible winners while turning one automatic winner into a possible loser. So most players thought it was a better game. But its actually much worse. The house edge is about three times as much. Do you see why? Turning 2,3, and 12 into points is no big deal because they will probably still lose. Meanwhile you are also turning eleven into a point. So it goes from a sure winner to a probable loser.

The precise house edge is easy to calculate if you can add and multiply fractions like you are taught in fifth grade. But Bob like everyone else in the casino business at that time, didn't realize this. So when I quickly gave him the answer that matched up with some professor he had hired, he was impressed enough to invite me to lunch the next day to discuss a possible deal.

When I went to my appointment at his place, I found Vegas World surprisingly busy. There were two reasons. One had to do with a nationwide promotion that I would be learning about in more detail down the road. The other one I was already vaguely familiar with. A game that Bob called Double Exposure 21. Blackjack where both the dealer's hole cards are exposed. In return for this edge the dealer won ties and paid even money rather than 3-2, on blackjack. The public was going crazy over this game. Hi rollers from Caesar's Palace were taking limousines down to this dumpy little casino to bet $500 a hand. Almost everyone felt that the compensation from ties and even money naturals was not enough to make up for the knowledge of the hole card. And the normal reason to avoid a game "If they didn't have an edge the casino wouldn't offer it." didn't apply here because people assumed that Bob was capable of screwing up.

But he hadn't. Perfectly played basic strategy gave you a very small edge. But almost everyone played far from perfectly. Bob was making millions. The game hadn't enticed me because I knew the relevant statistics. Remember that a few years earlier I had played essentially the same game, without the drawbacks, when I was catching hole cards. And I knew that the theoretical edge of front loading was in the ten percent range (ignoring insurance which doesn't apply here) if you made no effort to disguise yourself. I also knew that Bob's winning ties and even money BJ payoff was about ten percent for him. So it wiped the edge from knowing the hole card, out. It took about a year for people to wise up to Double Exposure and Crapless Craps (with the help of newspaper and magazine articles). But it was fun while it lasted.

(Note: Years later most people thought that I had come up with both Double Exposure 21 and Crapless Craps for Vegas World. And I did in fact come up with lots of ideas that made Bob a lot of money, some of which I'll tell you about in later chapters. But not those two games. Bob found them on his own and I want to set that record straight.)

At our lunch Bob started off by asking me to teach him poker. I agreed but then went on to tell him that I could be useful in many decision making situations besides gambling math. He asked me about a decision he was facing regarding his use of gifts for his customers. And when I quickly gave him a solution, he decided that he wanted me on his team in some kind of way. Even before deciding on exactly what I might do for him, he offered me a full comp (room and food) at his hotel anytime I wanted it and dubbed me his "Resident Wizard." I still have my business cards with that description.

Chapter Twenty-one: Thoughts Part 2

Here are some more ideas indirectly related to gambling or poker thinking.

1.   When it is time to sell something, don't be unduly influenced by the amount you paid for it
and whether it results in a profit or loss. If you got it cheaply don't be satisfied with a nice
profit if it could very well fetch you more. Conversely don't hold on to something that is now
clearly worth less than you paid for it. If you can get a reasonable price for it given your new
opinion, don't be influenced by the fact that your transaction finalizes your loss. (Of course,
tax considerations might sometimes change things but only if its close.)

2.   Be aware that when deciding between two or more actions, that the action that is most likely
to turn out best need not be the one you should choose. There are three ways this could
happen. The other action(s) is slightly less likely to be best but when it is, there is a good
chance it has a big upside that the other alternatives don't. Or the action with the best chance
to be best has a better chance to wind up catastrophically wrong than the other alternatives.
Or an action that is less likely to be right can be reversed if it fails, while the others can't.

3.   There are some things in life (or poker) that are very sensitive to slight changes in
parameters. They are susceptible to what is now called the "butterfly effect". If you think you
are dealing with something like that you are quite likely to come to a wrong decision if there
is some small piece of information you are lacking as that one piece might very well change

your decision. This is especially relevant if you are in some sort of competition with someone who may be in possession of that piece.

4.   There are some times in life where a profitable decision for big money should temporarily be passed up because your expected value increases further if you wait a bit longer to make sure that nothing happens to change your mind. A blackjack analogy occurs if you know the dealer's hole card, ties tie, you have eleven and the dealer has 17 which he will stand on. If you double down (where you get only one card) you win that extra bet if you catch a 7,8,9,T,J,Q,or K while losing if you catch an A,2,3,4,or 5. You are about an 7-5 favorite. In spite of that, doubling down is the wrong play. Because if you don't, you sometimes catch a bad card and still win with one or more further hits. That doesn't happen that often but when it does it is a THREE bet swing. You win one bet rather than losing two. In other words, if you regret not doubling down it is because the decision cost you one bet. If you regret doubling down it is sometimes because it costs you one bet but also sometimes because it costs you three bets. The math says see another card rather than doubling down. I'll leave it to you to think of where such situations might occur in your own life.

5.   After an NFL touchdown, a kicked extra point is close to 100 percent to succeed. A two point running or passing conversion is a little over 40 percent. A one pointer has a slightly higher EV. But sometimes that doesn't matter and the two point try is clearly better. For instance with little time remaining and your touchdown puts you up by one. But there are other times, not nearly as obvious, where the two point try is mathematically correct. Here is one that almost all coaches get wrong. Again, it is near the end of the game when you score a TD.

Except this time, you are down by eight. Furthermore, you team is about equal to the opponent and is assumed to be about even money if it goes to overtime. To make the math simple let's call the one point conversion 100 percent and the two pointer 40 percent. (If those assumptions make the two pointer better, the real world percentages make it better still.)

The calculations assume that you will score one more touchdown. You probably won't but if you don't, none of this matters. If you go for one on your first touchdown you will be seven points behind and if you score again you will obviously take the one point again and go into overtime. That makes you 50 percent. If instead you go for two the first time, you will go for two again if you missed and take the one (and the win) if you made the two. So assuming you score twice, a two point try after the first score gives you a total probability of winning of 40 percent plus 60 percent (missed the first try) x 40 percent (made the second) x 50 percent (won in overtime). That's 52 percent. A two percent improvement which, in real life is probably greater given the statistics.

6.   When people try to dispute conclusions based on mathematical analysis by invoking psychology or other such things, take that with a major grain of salt when you know that they didn't originally know the math. Many coaches when confronted with #5 above and other mathematical results, (such as when to punt or when to bunt) tried to say that the mathematicians were wrong because they didn't take into account things like the idea that teams would be demoralized if they missed the first two pointer. I would be much more inclined to give that credence if the coach was previously aware of the math and made the

decision to override it. But of course that is rarely the case. It's hard to believe that pros are so susceptible to demoralization that it would overcome the higher mathematical chances of going for two. Much easier for me to believe that the coaches were belatedly trying to rationalize their ignorance.

Chapter Twenty-two: 29 Million Lost. My Sad Story About Caribbean Stud

It is normally very difficult, expensive, and time consuming to get a new table game into Vegas casinos. If you think you have invented a good game you first need to get one of them to agree to put the game on the floor on a trial basis and agree to keep careful track of how it does for 60 days. If you have their promise you then need to get permission from the gaming commission to do that. Which requires you to have all the math of the game worked out and verified plus other relevant information. If you get through all that and there is no problem with the trial, the gaming commission will give you permission to rent or sell the game to other casinos. Normally the original casino gets it for free in return for what they did for you. However, that is rarely enough incentive for them to go to the trouble that a trial entails.

But as Resident Wizard of Vegas World and someone who was becoming a personal buddy to Bob Stupak, I knew it would be a lot easier than usual to negotiate the obstacle course that casino game inventors normally have to deal with. If I came up with a good game, Bob would put it on trial and help me with everything I would need to do if the game worked. So I set my mind to thinking up a new casino table game. The year was 1982.

Naturally my first thought was a table game based on poker. People told me that there was no way to do that but to me that just meant that I would unlikely have competition in creating a poker table game. The approach I took was the same I subsequently took when creating other games. Base the game on a math principle. And in this case, I realized that the math principle should be Game Theory calling strategy. One example of that would be that if it is the last round of betting, it is normally correct to call a pot size bet half of the time. When facing such a strategy there is no good decision as to whether to bluff the size of the pot when your had can't win a showdown. If the poker hand is simply five cards dealt with no draw, and the bet must be the size of the pot, then game

theory says to call that bet with a pair or better, plus AK high.

To recreate that scenario on a casino table was simple. The player and the dealer both ante

say, a dollar. (The dealer doesn't physically ante since he is matching various size antes from the

players at the table. If he loses, he settles up later.) The player and dealer are now dealt a five card

poker hand. If the player likes his hand or if he wants to "bluff" he matches the size of the "pot" ie

bets two dollars more. The dealer "calls" with AK high or better. So this is essentially a simplified

poker game. Except the player cannot "check". He must bet or fold. If he folds, he loses his dollar

even if he has the dealer beaten. This is a huge disadvantage. Other possibilities are that he bets the

two dollars (three dollars total) and beats the dealer out of only his one dollar "ante" because the

dealer has worse than AK. That's bad when the player is betting a good hand but good if the player is

bluffing. If the dealer "qualifies" with AK or better and the player bets into him, the better hand beats

the other hand out of three bucks.

So far this is a giant edge for the house. But that was fine because it allowed me to add

wrinkles that would make the game better and more interesting for the player while still maintaining

a small house advantage. One wrinkle was that the dealer exposed two of his cards, randomly of

course. This helped the player in two ways. First it saved him money if the two cards are AK or a

pair and he can't beat what he sees. Secondly a bluff becomes the correct play if both hole cards are

smaller than a king. But this didn't bring down the edge that much. To bring it down to an acceptable

level the obvious solution was to add bonuses for high hands. The better the hand the higher the

bonus. Obviously. I stress the word "obviously" because that word made the difference of almost a

million dollars to me. I will explain shortly.

The game did well when it was on trial. But during that time two bad things happened. Actually, one bad and one terrible. The bad thing was that when I went to an attorney to try to patent it, he claimed that such games could not be patented. The best I could do was trademark the name which was "Casino Poker". I don't know to this day whether he was giving me accurate information. Many casino table games based on poker have since been patented. However, it is my understanding that there was a change in patent laws in the 1980s so maybe my lawyer was right at the time. In any case it didn't matter much because during that time Sherry died. This isn't an autobiography so I won't go into detail. Except to say that I no longer felt like going through with the stuff that needed to be done to get the game out to the public, especially given the fact that the income would be small since I couldn't patent it.

Several years went by. Then one day a Vegas poker grinder named James approached me and asked me to give him some details about Casino Poker. He had played it a few times but didn't really remember the rules. The reason he was asking was that a guy he knew, Danny Jones, had bought a small casino in Aruba, a tiny island country just north of Venezuela. James was hoping that he could persuade Danny to put the game in his casino, have it become a success, and pocket some money. He suggested that he and I fly down there and split whatever reward Danny gave us if the game worked. Flying thousands of miles to another country in the hopes that a small casino owner would make a lot of money and give me some of it did not appeal to me. So instead I told James that I would explain the game in detail to him and if he somehow earned good royalties from the trip he made without me, he could toss me something up to a maximum of $15,000.

More years passed. Then one day someone mentioned that they saw my game on a cruise ship. I soon learned it was on several cruise ships. But it wasn't called Casino Poker. It had been renamed Caribbean Stud. And it was apparently doing well. So, didn't James owe me some money? I investigated further and found out that the game in Aruba was so popular that Danny Jones was able to sell or rent it to the ships. I also learned that he had changed the rules a bit. He exposed one card rather than two, (which I thought was a bad idea). He also gave out high hand bonuses only if the dealer qualified with AK or better. Otherwise the base game was the same. But he also added something else. A one dollar optional side bet that paid a huge jackpot for a Royal Flush, a big jackpot for a straight flush, and nice money for other good hands. And that Royal Flush jackpot was "progressive". It kept increasing until it hit. Sometimes it went over $100,000. Furthermore, the jackpot amount was flashing and increasing on a big display at the table.

It is quite possible that the dollar side bet and the progressive jackpot was a big reason for the game's success. (The other two rules changes were irrelevant.) I'll admit that right now. And in any case, I had abandoned the game a long time ago. So it didn't bother me that this fellow Danny Jones, who I had never met, was doing well with it. But if he had made a deal with James where was my 15K.? I was also a little irked that he got a patent on the game. Irked at my lawyer that is. Not Danny. Because it was too late for me. If you invent something but don't begin a patent process within one year, you are out of luck. But that means that if you are careless and then someone (illegally) patents the same invention a few years later, perhaps because he happened to see your invention previously, you have no incentive to do anything about it. (Except of course if you want to reduce the gizmo's price to the public. Or if you want to blackmail the patent holder. But that wasn't my thing. I just wanted my damn money from James.)

And I wanted it even more when the game received approval in Nevada and elsewhere in the US. Danny was making millions. And I found out that James had made six figures. But I also found out that James was, shall we say, "irresponsible" and never really had the money to pay me what he admitted he owed me.

Then one day in the year 2000 or thereabouts I am at some sort of gaming show where people were exhibiting their wares. And there was Danny Jones. We still had never met. But he knew who I was. I went up to him to complain about James. He was completely unaware of our deal. So he said "get lost, it's not my problem." Do you believe that? Hopefully you didn't. Actually, what happened is that he reached into his pocket and gave me fifteen thousand dollars in cash. We chatted briefly and since he was a casino owner, I suggested that perhaps I could be a part time consultant. He was amenable and I asked for $2000 a month.

A few weeks later I had a meeting with him and his lawyer where they were asking me about Casino Poker's high hand bonuses. I didn't know why and didn't want to know. But I was to eventually find out.

I collected money from Danny for a year or two plus he paid for me to get a patent on another game which I called Holdem Challenge. I'll describe that briefly later. We were supposed to split the profits but instead he sold me his half for a dollar! Pretty generous considering that I later sold two thirds of the rights to that game for over $100,000. But he could afford to be generous. Because a few months later he sold Caribbean Stud to Mikohn Gaming for THIRTY MILLION DOLLARS.

About a year later I get a call from Mark Yoseloff who was the CEO of Shufflemaster (and also a PhD in math). They made shuffle machines and had recently gotten into the table game business. We knew each other a little bit because we were in discussions about Holdem Challenge. But this call wasn't about that. Rather it was about a lawsuit. Mikohn was suing them because of Shufflemaster's game Let It Ride. The game itself wasn't the problem. Rather it was the fact that Let it Ride offered a one dollar side bet that could win a big jackpot just like Caribbean Stud. And Mikohn had just bought the patent on that dollar bet. Danny had actually obtained two patents all those years ago. One was on the game and one was on the side bet. Since Casino Poker had no side bet, what was the problem?

The problem was that the two patents were somewhat connected. If it was determined that the game patent was incorrectly granted due to an erroneous patent application, the side bet patent could still remain. But not if the errors in the game patent application were KNOWINGLY erroneous.

The original patent application for Caribbean Stud did in fact mention Casino Poker. But it claimed that it was sufficiently different to deserve a patent because Casino Poker, unlike their game, did not offer high hand bonuses. (Caribbean Stud offered high hand bonuses aside from those that required the side bet.) But of course my game did include bonuses. The patent office believed them without investigating. If the patent office was ever apprised of this error the game patent would be gone. But that was no big deal. The dollar side bet patent was the prize. And that would only go away (which would save Shufflemaster) if it could be proven that Danny KNEW that my original game had bonuses. And since it was common knowledge that he learned of the game from James and since James claimed that he had not told Danny about my bonuses (because I supposedly forgot to tell him), Danny could reasonably claim that not mentioning them on the application was an honest mistake. That's why I got a phone call. And an invitation to stop by Shufflemaster's office. For some reason my brain was kind of foggy that first meeting. I realized that I needed to find out if Danny could be forced to give back his $30,000,000. When he said no I resumed discussions with Shufflemaster. (NOTE: until all this came down, I had no idea about these patent technicalities and certainly had no legal obligation to divulge details of my game to anyone.) I told them I had no problem testifying at a deposition hearing and by the way could you use a consultant? You can pay me with stock options even though the stock might go to zero if you lose the lawsuit. They were nice enough to say yes.

73

At the deposition I was not willing to say that I was certain that I had remembered explaining the bonuses to James. But I did say that it seemed inconceivable that I hadn't. Furthermore I offered the expert opinion that it was (or at least should be) OBVIOUS to any casino that the original game had bonuses because without them, the game's giant edge would have insured failure (and probably wouldn't even have been allowed to go on trial). The deposition lasted hours but that was the bottom line. My mathematical reasoning convinced Mikohn that they could not convince a juror that Danny's erroneous application was an honest mistake. So they settled. Shufflemaster, I believe, paid them a pittance so that Mikohn would not be forced let the world know about their problem and could claim they won. But in real life Shufflemaster won. And after selling my options I made about a million, Or, if you'd rather, lost $29 million.

Chapter Twenty-three: Three Bracelets. Sort Of

As I've said several times, this isn't really an autobiography. Almost everything I'm writing in this book is stuff that I think might be useful for the reader. But there are a few exceptions. Some juicy stories that name big names or the occasional biographical anecdote that would seem odd to leave out. Like my three World Series of Poker wins. Two in 1982 and one in 1983. All three were in games that are no longer tournament events. The 1982 events were Mixed Doubles, where you and you opposite sex partner switch every 30 minutes, and Draw Poker. My mixed doubles partner was Dani Kelly. The game was seven card stud. I don't remember anything interesting or educational about that tournament. The Draw game was not Jacks or better. It had a big blind and an ante. There were two notable things about that tournament. One was that I was dealt a pat royal flush in the big blind and got a walk! In other words, everyone folded. I won only the antes with the royal yet it didn't hurt me one bit, because I won the tournament. Not something you see every day.

More relevant was the play when the game became heads up. This was a limit game and if you were first to act you either folded or made a bet that happened to be the size of the pot. My opponent played way too tight. He needed two sevens or better to call an opening bet. That occurs only about 35 percent of the time. Getting even money on a 65 percent shot was such an insane edge that it would have been wrong to risk losing a lot of money on any one hand almost no matter how good it was. It was a near certainty that I would grind him down through ante steals. Unless he wised up. Which made me think about a poker tactic that I have written about many times since. Namely that if you are lucky enough to find an opponent who is making a very bad mistake don't take ultimate advantage of it if that risks him realizing his error. My theoretically correct strategy was to open 100 percent of my hands against this fellow. But if I did, he was almost certainly smart enough to bring his calling criteria well below sevens. I opened about 80 percent of my hands and the result was a foregone conclusion.

There was something unique about the 1982 tournament. Up until then the event winners received, besides the money, a very nice gold bracelet inscribed with your name and the event. The gold itself was worth about $1000. And of course, the actual collector's value was higher. But for some reason Binion's decided to switch in 1982. Perhaps because what they switched to was worth a lot more. It was a gold Baume Mercier watch with a cover over the watch face that could be pulled open like some of the old time pocket watches. I believe I am the only one with two of them. Inscribed of course. If I ever go broke, I Think I could get at least 25K for each but hopefully I'll never need to find out.

The 1983 tournament I won was in limit Omaha. It replaced the Draw event. And the watch was replaced as well. In spite of its lesser value, the bracelet had become iconic and the players wanted it back. But this one didn't measure up. Binion's chose a local poker playing jeweler to make them and they weren't as nice or as big as the previous ones. So he wasn't asked to provide them again in 1984. And I had yet another trophy that was given out only one year.

The tournament itself was not memorable. But it was kind of cool that I was prevented from defending my championship and went on to win the tourney replacing it. But then they did it to me again! Limit Omaha was offered just that one year and was replaced by Pot Limit Omaha in 1984. Could I throw a second monkey wrench in these conspirator's desire to keep me from winning yet again? I'm sure they were pulling their hair out when it got down to two of us with almost equal chips. More so when I got all in with three deuces when the flop came AK2. He had AK. The river was a king.

Chapter Twenty-four: Two Small Feuds With Gambling/Math Experts

After I wrote my first book, I signed on with a magazine called Gambling Times to write a

monthly column about all aspects of gambling. (Almost all of them were reprinted in my book

Getting The Best of It.) Most of their other writers were nothing special. But one certainly was.

Edward Thorp. The author of Beat the Dealer. And a PhD in math.

One month there was a letter to the editors asking Thorp about a curious statistic in his book.

It stated that a blackjack player who is somehow playing against a 36 card deck that contains four of

each rank but no tens or picture cards, has a small advantage. How is that possible he asked. Beat the

Dealer contained a chart regarding "depleted decks". It gave the player's advantage or disadvantage

when playing perfect basic strategy against decks that had one category of card missing. If an

otherwise normal deck had no fives that was a nice advantage for the player. If it contained no nines

it was a disadvantage. But the perfect basic strategy was NOT normal basic strategy. Rather it was

the best strategy against that particular depleted deck. In other words, before coming up with the

house edge, the computer calculated a new optimum strategy and assumed that the player was

following it. (But it didn't assume that the player was "counting" and altering strategy based on cards

played.) The book made that clear. But it did not actually tell you what those ten different basic

strategies were.

Even if you played ordinary 52 card deck basic strategy you would have an edge if you were

playing against a 48 card deck containing no fives. That edge doesn't increase by much if you play

the fiveless basic strategy But against a deck a with no ten value cards, strategy changes, whatever

they might be, clearly must help you a real lot compare to normal strategy. Because without those

tens how could you be anywhere near an even game using regular basic strategy? You would be doing things like doubling down on nine against a four and standing on 13 against a 3. Which are obviously terrible plays against a tenless deck. When you add that to the fact that you will be dealt zero blackjacks it becomes ridiculous to think normal basic strategy could give you an edge. In fact, it would result in a giant disadvantage. Isn't that completely obvious?

Well apparently, it wasn't obvious to Thorp. Because his reply, as near as I can remember it, was "The edge you saw cited in the book was not assuming the player played normal basic strategy. Rather the computer played the basic strategy it calculated for a tenless deck. If you played normal basic strategy against such a deck, I doubt you would have an edge." I couldn't believe he wrote that third sentence. He merely "doubted" it. Said differently he only thought that normal basic strategy "probably" wouldn't win. I blasted him for not giving it any thought and evidently blindly looking at his computer results without contemplating them. He did not take kindly to the criticism.

Meanwhile getting back to that tenless deck. What kind of possible basic strategy can beat it? Think about it. It's really not that hard to come up with it once you are told that the player does indeed have an edge. Remember that there are no blackjacks, double downs are rarely if ever right, and splits are a tiny factor if they help at all. Obviously, you will hit more stiffs than normal. But the dealer hits up to 16. And if you play exactly like the dealer, he has an edge since you go first and therefore, he wins when you both bust (or, when playing heads up, he would have busted). Take a minute to think. I'll wait.

The answer of course is that if you have an edge it must be because you will often hit hard 17! Actually, you always would hit it. Standing with it is much worse for you than it would be

78

against a normal deck. And hitting it is nowhere near as bad as it would normally be. I will never

think that Thorp not knowing that, was anything other than unforgiveable.

Stanford Wong, another PhD, delved into many gambling games besides blackjack. His

book on tournaments was excellent. And so was his book on horse racing. Except for one sentence.

Like Thorp he forgot to think. But unlike Thorp he had a chance to correct his mistake before he

wrote it and instead compounded it by not believing me. The subject was Pick Sixes and other bets of

that nature. You pick the winner of six races and if you win all six, you win lots of money. If no one

does that, some of the money bet is added to the jackpot for the next day. If no one wins that, it

increases still further. At some point the jackpot gets high enough that a player could have a

mathematical edge if he bets two bucks on one reasonable combination. Even though the track has

been raking about 20 percent from the pool. If his $2 ticket has a one in 80,000 chance of winning

and the jackpot is $200,000, he may have positive EV. But not for sure. It would depend on the

chance there will be another winning ticket. If there was (exactly) one, he would have to split it and

he would be getting only about 50,00 to 1 on an 80,000 to 1 shot.

When these things started springing up at a lot of tracks, wealthy gamblers started beating

them by betting on tens of thousands of reasonable combinations. Sometimes hundreds of thousands.

Usually just the minimum amount on each of them. They would wait until the "carryovers" brought

the jackpot past a certain amount and then they would strike. This was becoming so widespread that

the small bettors started to complain.

During this time, sometime in the 1990's, Stanford Wong wrote a horseracing manuscript

which he sent to other gambling authors, including me, asking for their opinions. In the manuscript

he addressed Pick Six type betting and the complaints of the small bettors. He wrote something like

"If these syndicates make thousands of $2 bets and indeed do have positive EV, then it logically means that a smaller subset of these bets must also have a positive EV. So all you need to do is find them, bet them, and not worry about the syndicates." How could that be wrong? If ten numbers average above 100 then you can find a smaller group from among them that averages over 100. But he was wrong. Do you see it? I'll wait again.

If we use small numbers it is easy to see. Suppose instead of millions of combos there are only ten, all almost equally likely. One of them is 11percent. For simplicity we will ignore the rake. There is a ten dollar carryover. The syndicate bets $2 on each combo and if no one else bets, they get back $30 for a ten dollar profit Now let's say that you, after reading Wong's statement, decide to bet because he says that if the syndicate has the best of it with multiple bets, some subset of their bets do too. You pick the slightly better 11 percent shot. About eight out of nine times you lose $2. Once out of nine times you split the $32 in the pot which gives you a $14 profit. Uh oh. You just got only 7-1 on an 8-1 shot. (Meanwhile, the syndicate now wins $12 eight times and loses $4 once.) What Wong didn't realize is that your bet can turn a profitable subset into an unprofitable one (while increasing the EV of the others). So, the little guys were in fact right that the syndicates who bet so many combinations as to insure you would split with them if you won, did in fact keep you from finding winning bets.

It was a significant error that I found, both because it affected readers actions and because he made a math/ logic mistake that would embarrass him. I thought that I deserved recognition in the text of his book. Not just in the acknowledgements section. I told him that I found a major error that deserved recognition within the text. He refused. He wrote the book with the error. I divulged it. And I never heard from him again.

Chapter Twenty-five: Two More Surprising Replies From Casino Big Shots

I'm sprinkling in a few anecdotes like these throughout this book even though they are not apt to teach you anything or even entertain you that much. For instance, that Sid Wyman story. But because they involve some pretty well-known names in Las Vegas history, and I am probably the only one who knows these tidbits, it's worth retelling them if only because one of them might attract the attention of the media and increase the chances you read (and learn) from this book.

In the late 70's Bobby Baldwin was probably the best No Limit Holdem player in the world. So, it was no surprise that he won Binion's World Series of Poker main event in 1978. But he was not the typical professional poker. To put it simply he was classier. Both in dress and demeaner. Plus he was a college graduate. That attracted the attention of Steve Wynn, the owner of the Golden Nugget at the time (before he became the multibillionaire who built the Mirage, the Bellagio, and the Wynn). Steve hired Bobby shortly after his win and made no secret of the fact that he was grooming him to run the place. He got his wish and Bobby Baldwin has gone on to run the Mirage, the Bellagio and as of this writing, the Aria.

But he almost didn't. When it came time to promote Bobby to the Nugget's CEO it was required that he get permission from the majority of the nine members of the Nevada Gaming Commission. But it is a two step process. First the application must be voted on by three of those members who were called the Nevada Control Board. And the rules were that if those three were unanimously against, you were essentially toast because the only way you could now be approved would be if the Commission vote two weeks later was UNANIMOUS the other way.

And Bobby had a problem. It was something along the lines of him being involved with an illegal poker game in Tulsa Oklahoma, where he was from. The details don't matter. Bobby denied it. I remember thinking that he could have claimed that what was alleged was no big deal but he didn't do that. He claimed complete innocence. I also recollect that most poker players thought he was probably guilty, but that with Steve Wynn behind him, it wouldn't matter. The Control Board did some investigation and then shocked the casino industry by turning Bobby down three to zero. Two weeks later he was approved unanimously. I have no idea what happened to change their mind. But that is not the subject of this anecdote. Rather it is about something Bobby said to me a few hours after he was turned down by the Board.

Although Bobby and I were not close friends I was something like an esteemed colleague who he was honest with. And when I happened to bump into him shortly after the decision, I felt like I should bring it up. He was very distraught. So to be polite, I pretended that I had no doubt about his innocence. I asked, "do you think those guys knew you were innocent and purposely lied when they stated otherwise, or were they instead confused by the evidence and came to the incorrect conclusion by mistake?" Almost certainly a guilty person would have chosen option #2. And probably, so would most innocent ones. But Bobby replied. "They knew the truth. They knew I was innocent. They purposely screwed me." Or words to that effect.

The second anecdote occurred several years later, shortly after I testified for the National Gaming Impact Study Commission. Terri Lanni CEO of MGM, was on the panel so when I saw him walking through his casino, I approached him even though we had never officially met. After chatting for a few minutes, I asked, "what do you think would happen to the casino business if Probability was made a required course in high school?" He didn't say "not much" or "we would be hurt a bit but people will always want to gamble". He said "We would all have to close our doors." Another shocking answer. Shocking partially because he was smart enough to realize what is almost certainly true (The few times I have given casino tours to math teacher they are baffled that anyone is playing the games) and partially because he was willing to admit it to me. An admission that the

industry he had made his career, was wholly dependent on ignorance. Ignorance that if it didn't exist,

would make the world a much better place.

Chapter Twenty-six: Some Early Ideas For Stupak

My Resident Wizard status for Bob was interrupted after a couple of years by the legalization of holdem and stud in California cardrooms. Most of the best schemes I came up with for him occurred after I came back in about 1987, and will be mentioned later. Plus, an amazing revelation. But there were a few interesting things that happened in those first few years (besides giving him general advice during our almost daily lunches) that are worth repeating here. Most were already discussed in DUCY so even though you might find one of them helpful I won't go into as much detail as I did in that book.

1.   The first day of work I suggested to Bob that employees were doing the bare minimum to get their paycheck. To prove it I put a newspaper on the floor of the casino and overturned a chair a few feet from the bar. Dozens of employees walked by without picking either up. Bob was watching from a distance and was livid. When questioned they claimed it was the porter's job.

2.   Our special packages meant that the front desk was very busy four days a week and almost empty the other three. But our front desk employees needed to be paid what amounted to about $100 a day, five days a week. So the slow days were highly overstaffed. The wasted money was insignificant but I found a simple win win method to make everyone happy and save a few hundred bucks a week. An extra day off wasn't worth taking if it meant losing a day's pay. But for some it was worth it if they only lost half that. Just enough people accepted $450 for a four day week to balance the schedule out. (Had that not been true in

85

either direction we would have tweaked the offer.) Again, the money was almost irrelevant. but the general technique could undoubtedly be applied in many situations

3.   Our sports book got "middled" several times. We had moved the football line a half a point based on the bets we were booking, and when the result landed on the number, most of the bettors either won or pushed. In some cases, a half point move is unwise. But so is not moving the line and getting highly unequal action. So I told Bob to keep the pointspread the same but move the moneyline away from 11-10. If a three point favorite is getting most of the action move it to minus 120 - even or minus 130-plus 110. My solution is now used by everyone but I believe we were the first.

4.   With Double Exposure on the wane, Bob asked me to come up with another variation for his 21 tables. My answer was a game we called Experto 21 There were two underlying ideas that helped me create that game. Many players fancy themselves winning "counters" even though they have no right to. And people underestimate the strength of the house paying only even money on a natural blackjack even the though calculation is ridiculously simple ($16/52 \times 4/51 \times 2$). If you are good enough to play normal blackjack to a standstill you will lose 2 1/2 percent of your action playing Experto. Thus, my idea was to offer a single deck game dealt down to the next to last card, that paid even money on a blackjack. (Next to last, otherwise we would open ourselves to something called "endplay".) That game lasted the life of his casino.

Chapter Twenty-seven: Jeff Yass: From Poker Pro To Billionaire

Stock options are interesting little creatures. Especially to us math geeks. For those who don't know how they work, here is a quick primer.

Say it is September 21 and XYZ stock closed at $40. If you are rather sure the stock will go up you can buy it and if you think the opposite you can "short" it. If you have $400 to play with you can buy or short ten shares (if you don't want to go into debt).

(From this point forward I will, for simplicity's sake, speak only of the investments that hope the stock will go up. Stock options in that category are called "calls". (There are also mirror image investments and the stock option involved is called a "put". But I will not get into them in this mini lesson. If this chapter piques your interest you can investigate further.)

If you buy XYZ at 40 and it goes to 60 in a month you made 50 percent on your money. But suppose you thought that there was a good chance this would happen, (perhaps because of some news item,) but also a good chance the stock will go down somewhat. Is there some way you can turn such an opinion, (assuming its accurate,) and your $400 into a higher EV than a simple buy of the stock will do? Yes. Stock options. In this case "calls".

Calls are basically a piece of paper that promises to let you buy a share of stock (if you want) for a specified period of time, anytime until the expiration date. They usually come in many flavors, combining different "strike prices" with different expiration dates. Here are four hypothetical examples for XYZ.

A.   The option to buy XYZ for $45 anytime up to October 27.

B.   The option to buy XYZ for $45 anytime up to December 15.

C.   The option to buy XYZ for $35 anytime up to December 15

D.   The option to buy XYZ for $15 anytime up to December 15.

These pieces of paper with these promises cost money. The owner of XYZ is not going to allow you to buy XYZ anytime in the next five weeks, even for the $45 that will give him a profit, unless he gets something for that promise. Otherwise it's a freeroll for you. You lose nothing if the price never exceeds 45 and if it does you can buy it cheap (and, if you choose, immediately sell it). So what would be in it for him? Thus, you have to pay something.

The fair price for an option to buy a stock for $45 anytime in the next five weeks, that is presently selling for $40, depends on a few things. But the main one is the stock's volatility. Suppose for instance that the present $40 price is based on somehow knowing that it is even money to be $50 in five weeks and 50 percent to be $30. Buying the stock gives you a short term EV of $0. But Option A, if it was free, would be profitable. Half the time you would "exercise" it for 45 and make five bucks. Half the time you would let it go. So your EV would be $2.50. And that $2.50 would be the fair price to pay for that call. But it would be different if the stock was known to be even money to be either 55 or 25 in five weeks. The stock's EV is still 40 but the call is now worth $5.00 ($10 half the time.) Obviously in real life it's a lot more complicated.

Option B must be worth more than Option A. Because it allows you to do anything Option A allows while giving the stock more time to get above the strike price.

Option C is a call that is "in the money". If you owned it you could immediately buy the stock for 35 and sell it for 40. So its worth at least $5. But it's actually worth more. In the less volatile scenario above its worth $7.50. In the more volatile scenario, its worth $10. The reason its value is not simply 40 minus 35 is the limited downside of the call compared to the downside you would have if you bought the stock. Option D, however is different. The fair price is simply $25 (40-15) because the stock will almost never go below $15 so the option gives you very little downside protection.

Obviously, anyone who fully understands this stuff has a nice edge when he is dealing with someone who doesn't. Here are three other aspects to options trading that helps experts vs amateurs

1.   There are opportunities for "middles" similar to those in sports betting. Sometimes those middles make a profit a sure thing. This could happen because some combination of more than one option or an option combined with the underlying stock results in a little or no risk investment.

2.   If you deem a stock to have a positive EV the option associated with it could be more profitable even if the EV per option is smaller because you can usually buy a lot more of them for the same amount of money.

3.   Starting about 1975, exchanges were set up to make it much easier to sell a call (or put), including those you didn't own, as well as buy them. And that could be done any time before the expiration date. Thus, those with the requisite expertise could formulate all kinds of profitable strategies.

Jeff Yass got in near the ground floor of these new opportunities when he was about 25 years old. He moved to Chicago, traded options and soon thereafter started Susquehanna Securities. Now he is worth about a billion dollars. But in 1980 he was a struggling professional poker player who was studying my early books. One day he approached me with a seven card stud problem. After I answered him, he asked "what if it was 8 card stud?". Even though there was no such game.

Years later Jeff offered me two opportunities. He actually paid me several thousand dollars to fly to Chicago and let him try to persuade me to become an options trader for his company. He also gave me a nice offer to analyze the stats of an NFL team whose owner was his friend. I turned them both down. The football proposition was too much work. The options job meant I had to wear a tie. However, the money he spent flying me out there was not wasted. Because I showed him something related to the Stanford Wong error mentioned earlier. Jeff was one of those guys beating Pick Six carryovers by betting mega combinations. But he overestimated how big the carryover had to be in order to have a nice edge. (In fact if there was no rake a syndicate would have an edge even if there was zero carryover). This non intuitive fact arises from the fact that the combinations bet are not random. Rather they are picked with the criteria that they never duplicate each other. I won't go into detail but suffice it to say that Jeff starting shooting at pick sixes that he previously passed on. And, I believe made a lot more than the cost of my trip.

Although this chapter is fairly long, the main reason I wrote it was to mention his question about 8 card stud. The fact that he realized that a purely hypothetical question could give him insight into real life questions. Lots of people pooh pooh such questions. But I doubt many billionaires do. That's the lesson for this chapter. To this day, as far as I know, Susquehanna requires that all their financially related employees read my book Getting The Best of It. They have bought thousands of them. So maybe that's a second lesson.

Chapter Twenty-eight: More Thoughts

Here are some not as related to gambling.

1. **Be suspicious of products that benefit from the placebo effect.** You probably hear a lot of radio commercials for various vitamins or supplements where the first shipment is almost free. Don't assume that their willingness to offer that promotion means they are legitimate. Enough people convince themselves that they feel better, have less pain, don't have to pee, or whatever, to reorder stuff that is pretty worthless (unless you are susceptible to the placebo effect yourself.)

2. **Generous annuities should be offered to the unhealthy.** Especially to those who can prove they have a terminal disease. Right now, as far as I know, monthly payments that last until you are dead, are completely unacceptable to those whose life expectancy don't correspond to actuarial tables. So, if you have a medium size bankroll and a short but unclear life expectancy, the responsible strategy would be to keep your expenditures low enough so that you won't go broke if you are fortunate enough to live a few years longer than you thought you would. An annuity that pays a dividend more in line with the poor health of the prospective purchaser would probably be appreciated (since it would allow buyers to spend more per year than their frugal budget would have) while still, on average, making insurance companies a nice profit.

3.   **Equip all cars with a "Sorry Signal."** Most road rage occurs when the other driver does something wrong *unintentionally*. And most people's anger would quickly subside if that was quickly acknowledged. There should be an easily seen light or even a sign saying "sorry" that would light up with the push of a button.

4.   **Different deductions for charities.** Some charities are more worthwhile than others. Partly depending on what they do and partly depending on what percentage of the donated money gets to the people (or animals) that are being helped. Perhaps it would be a good idea to use tax incentives to encourage giving more to the good ones as opposed to the sketchy ones.

5.   **Intentional fouls should mean three free throws (rather than two) when up by three, near games end.** It just seems wrong that technically breaking the rules (fouling) should practically insure a win.

6.   Evolution supposedly occurs because genes sometimes mutate and the resultant plant or animal finds it easier to survive than its parents. Simplistically speaking. But apparently there are some species that seemed to have changed faster than would be expected based on the normal rate of mutations. Which leads me to wonder if there are perhaps something like 2nd derivate genes (that could also mutate). In other words, genes that control the rate of mutation of other genes.

Chapter Twenty-nine: More Ridiculous Casino Promotions and Mistakes

Here are some other ways I supplemented my poker income in Las Vegas in the 80's before book writing became a big part of my life.

1.   **Casinos paying 2-1 on a blackjack.** I have already mentioned how paying only even money rather than 3-2 in games like Double Exposure or Experto 21 added 2.5 percent to the casino's edge. Because of the easily calculated fact that you are dealt a natural about 5 percent of the time. But it goes the other way as well. Paying an extra half a bet means a player who normally skilled enough to play a break even strategy will now have a 2.5 percent edge. A good counter might achieve 4 percent. In spite of this casinos occasionally offered this game (likely because they didn't know how much they were giving away) and I was usually there when they did.

2.   **Plus EV progressive slot and poker machine jackpots.** Along with early surrender in Atlantic City, this was an opportunity that I was usually too lazy to take advantage of. A few people made over a million dollars by hiring teams of players to play these profitable machines. The few moderate scores I did make, I did on my own when I had some extra time on my hands.

        In a nutshell, the idea was to jump on machines that offered progressive jackpots that had increased to a certain point. Namely the point where the average number of pulls (or hands) that you played before you hit the symbol combination (or Royal Flush) that pays the jackpot, will have you being down less money than the jackpot will pay. Its not that easy to

94

determine the size that a slot machine progressive jackpot (meaning one that keeps increasing the longer it is not hit) has to be before its worth playing. But it is easy when it comes to poker machines. For example a typical quarter machine (that requires a $1.25 bet to be eligible) is paying back more than 100 percent if the initial $1000 jackpot has moved up to about $2500. Here's the problem though. Royal flushes occur approximately once every fifty hours. And you expect to be losing almost $2500 by the time you hit it (much more if you don't know how to draw correctly). So $3000 jackpots are worth only about ten dollars an hour. Thus, I never considered playing a quarter machine unless the jackpot hit 5k which was theoretically worth about $50 an hour. But those who were willing to have the headaches of hiring, firing, and training, typically paid their employees about ten dollars an hour and a $200 bonus if they hit the Royal. They had their team members shooting at jackpots of $3500 or so and, as I said, a few became millionaires.

This is still probably doable today. But its a lot harder for two reasons. One is that machines are usually set so that their progressive jackpots increase slower than they used to. So profitable machines are much rarer. The other problem is that a lot of people are now aware of profitable progressives, including those who are satisfied with minimum wage type pay. That means you can't wait, like I did, for the jackpot to get decently juicy. (I was sometimes able to because I knew about the concept before teams became widespread.)

3. **Blackjack and Craps Tournaments.** Just as in the horse betting tournament that I already told you about, the key to doing well in these tournaments was NOT being an expert in the game in question. Rather it was being able to deduce the important aspects of the tournament format. Stanford Wong goes into great detail in his book on the subject. But much of his

advice can be deduced with simple logic. For example, suppose the goal is to be ahead more money than anyone else at your blackjack table after 50 hands are dealt. It is the last hand. All but one of your opponents are too far back to matter. He is slightly behind you in chips. If you both bet the same amount and he stands with a 16 against a ten in front of you, then you should make the normally horrible play of standing with a 12. And of course, there are many much more complex tactics. Most of the entrants were clueless. Still, given the rake, the hourly EV was usually only moderate. So I didn't bother with most of them.

4.   **Correlated Parlay Cards.** All serious sports gamblers now know about them. But it wasn't always true. There was once a time where it was easy to find good bets on special parlay cards where all the bets offered involved propositions involving a single game. Usually the Super Bowl. And those propositions were sometimes not what mathematicians call "independent". But the payoffs were as if they were. For instance you could parlay your pick on which team kicks the first field goal, with which team kicked the most field goals. Ignoring ties, isn't it far more likely that the team that kicks the most field goals will be the one who kicks the first one?

There were numerous such dependent bets available on these one game parlay cards for many years. Some were less obvious and less profitable than the one I mentioned. But one was truly ridiculous. It was at the Bingo Palace. Three team parlay card bets paid 6-1 rather than the fair odds of 7-1. So did the special one game cards. And this particular card let you bet on which team won the first half (vs the spread of course. Again, ties were ties not losses.). You could also choose the winner of the second half. And you could make that a three proposition parlay by also betting on who won the game. Unless you want to claim that the winner of the first half is way over 50 percent to lose the second half, I think you can see

the bet here (actually two bets since you should take both sides).

5.   **The Rainbow Casino Birthday Promotion.** Appropriately this birthday promotion story

really took the cake. Once again I was perusing the paper just like I did when I came upon the

Stardust parlay card ad. And just like then, I did not really believe that the ad I was reading

could be true. In fact, it seemed even less likely. The parlay card eight out of ten fiasco, could

perhaps be explained by Vegas gamblers being ignorant of "combinatorics" as it doesn't

come up too often in Vegas games (except keno.) But there was no excuse for this error. The

ad claimed that the Rainbow Casino in Henderson, right outside Vegas, was celebrating their

birthday the next day, by giving something extra to their blackjack and craps players.`

Blackjack players would get 2-1 odds on their naturals. And craps players who bet the pass

line would be paid 3-2 odds if they won on their come out roll (as opposed to establishing a

point and then making it). In other words, if they bet that the shooter "passed" they would be

paid an extra half a bet if their first roll was a seven or an eleven.

They couldn't mean what the ad appeared to say. Unless they were perhaps restricting

these promotions to one or two dollar bets. (Normally their limit, as a small casino, was $50.)

And if somehow some clueless guy in marketing actually thought they could make this offer,

someone in the casino would surely rescind it. Maybe not the blackjack promotion. Most

people play that game badly enough that the extra 2.5 percent they were being given

wouldn't cost the Rainbow too much. But the craps promotion was a much different story. It

takes no skill to bet "pass". And it seemed inconceivable that they would actually pay what

the ad promised, to those who bet the limit. Why, because the underlying basic math was something that all dice personnel are supposed to know. Not to mention intelligent twelve year olds.

There are six ways to roll a seven. There are two ways to roll an eleven. There are 36 different ways to roll something. Eight out of 36 opening rolls are a seven or eleven. 22.2 percent. A pass line bettor playing at the Rainbow on its birthday would supposedly be paid an extra half a bet 22.2 percent of the time. The casino, which normally averages winning 1.4 percent of the amount bet is now adding 11.1 percent to the player. He now has an edge of 9.7 percent. A player betting fifty dollars a minute will average winning almost $300 an hour. A full craps table with such bettors would take the poor little Rainbow for about $100K before the night was over. That would be catastrophic for them. So it couldn't be true.

I called my buddy Jackie who had studied blackjack and moved out to Vegas to join me. We agreed to meet at the Rainbow shortly before the promotions were supposedly going to begin. I was very pessimistic about the craps game but the blackjack promotion was likely to be true, even for fifty dollar bets. When we got there the craps table was closed. I figured that was that. Rather than immediately ask them about the promotion, I decided it would be wiser to start playing blackjack and casually ask them about craps after we were playing awhile. They told me that it would open at 5PM, a few hours from then. Jackie and I had not let on that we were together so we met outside and I told him what they said. We went back to playing 21 at two different tables. Shortly thereafter the casino manager walks up to me and says, "sorry David you are too good for us" He was very friendly and even offered to buy me lunch. But I was barred from the blackjack game. I again met Jackie outside and told him to continue playing 21 on our combined bankroll but to of course switch to the craps table if and when they opened it. I told him to call me if that happened since it was possible that I wasn't barred from that game. (Counters who were backed off 21 were normally allowed to play the other games. But probably not in this case.)

Five o'clock rolls around with no call. Nor was there one at five thirty or six. It didn't make sense and I was ready to take a ride over there to see if something had gone wrong. Then Jackie called. The promotion was going on exactly as stated. He hadn't called because the table was packed with players and he didn't want to lose his spot. Finally, he got permission to go to the bathroom while they held his place so he was able to call me. He was already winning $500. He told me not to bother coming down because there was absolutely no room for me and people were waiting to squeeze in if someone left. Every player was betting $50 on the pass line and nothing else.

I decided to take a ride down there anyway just to see what was going on. I wouldn't let on that I knew Jackie in case that might make them bar him. When I got there the craps table was as smushed as Jackie described. With people waiting, there was no chance I could ever get to play, assuming I would even be allowed to. Still I got as close to the table as I could, just to watch. And the casino manager who had barred me earlier noticed me and approached me. When he reached me, he took me to the tables edge and announced to everyone that they had to find a way to squeeze together even closer so I could be allowed to play! He explained that he owed it to me because of something that had happened earlier. He barred me from a 3 percent edge and then went to great lengths to get me into a 10 percent edge game.

Jackie and I split up about $8000 after they finally closed up the game. If you think I am lying or embellishing this story I don't blame you. But I'm not.

Chapter Thirty: In The Middle of Larry Flynt's Alleged WSOP Attempted Fix

Hustler publisher Larry Flynt started to take an interest in poker around 1980. Nowadays he plays pretty well, especially seven card stud. But not back then. At no limit holdem he was barely better than a total beginner. A loose, aggressive playing beginner. One who had at least once, came to a game with a million dollars in cash in a briefcase. So it was no big deal for him to enter the ten thousand dollar buy in world championship tournament at Binion's Horseshoe in Las Vegas even though he realistically had no chance. In fact his chances were so miniscule that two time champ Doyle Brunson, laid Flynt a 1000 to 1 odds, a million dollars to a thousand, that he wouldn't win.

When the first day's play was over, Flynt was in the lead. It seemed hard to believe but not impossible. Very aggressive players sometimes get quite lucky in the short run. Meanwhile Flynt had made an appointment with me to visit him at his mega suite at the Aladdin Hotel that first evening, in order to get a last minute lesson. When I was there, I focused on him making a lot of preflop movins to "take the play out" of as many hands as possible. Especially when he was holding an ace. My lesson was not given secretly. In fact, Doyle had actually recommended me a few days earlier.

The second day I was actually playing at Larry's table. And on a couple of occasions after Larry moved in and won the pot, he flashed me an ace in his hand to show me that he had been paying attention. And his stack was continuing to move up. Doyle asked me whether I noticed anything suspicious and I said no. But aparently I was wrong.

Everything I have written so far is firsthand. What comes next is not. However it is "common knowledge" among the old high stakes player. In fact, I am told that Larry Flynt himself doesn't deny it and even jokes about it with those players that have since become his friends and play in his game at his Hustler casino in Gardena, California.

The scheme was supposedly hatched by Ken Smith, a notorious poker and chess expert from Texas, known for his black top hat. The idea was to bribe players who were at the same table as Flynt to dump chips to him. Supposedly they were offered the value of their chips plus ten thousand dollars more. Exactly how and when this scheme was discovered is not clear to me. But I do know that before the third day of the tournament, Doyle had a conversation of some sort with Larry and the bet was cancelled.

As for myself, I made $500 for an hour lesson but it may not have been worth it. Because there was probably some suspicion that I knew about the scheme and even perhaps was in on it. No one ever accused me of that, hopefully because Larry fully exonerated me. If he didn't, maybe he will do it now.

Chapter Thirty-one: Mason Malmuth's Friendly Takeover

When California legalized stud and holdem in the mid 80s, the pickings were too good to stay in Vegas. All those players used to playing draw and lowball had to now learn some new games. The Bicycle Club's major tournament that first year had me winning their overall championship. You still should be able to see my name above all the subsequent winners on the trophy they display. But aside from that, not much happened there that is worth repeating here. Except perhaps that it was during this time that I first met Mason Malmuth. I met him through Mike Caro, the man who wrote the Draw Poker section of Doyle Brunson's book. Mason was working as a statistician but he had become interested in poker. Mike had been giving him advice.

Shortly after meeting Mason, Bob Stupak made me an offer (including a new Thunderbird) if I were to return to Vegas and essentially become his second in command. The games in LA had become a bit tougher so I decided to accept. Lots of exploits and adventures would ensue and I will soon be telling you about many of them. But probably the most important incident that occurred when I went back to being Resident Wizard was a visit from Mason sometime in 1987 or thereabouts. He was not completely happy with what Mike Caro was telling him about limit holdem. Not surprising since Mike's game was Draw and he had played very little else. So Mason decided to hire me for some lessons. Over the next few weeks we sat in the coffee shop at Vegas World while I explained some fairly advanced concepts. Mason had asked me for permission to tape record the lessons and I agreed. Shortly thereafter Mason returned with a detailed summary of what he had recorded. Very detailed. He wanted to know whether he had accurately captured the main points of my lessons. When I read what he had written I realized that not only had he done a great job turning what I said into a written narrative, he essentially had the makings of a new book. One that would be more advanced and complete than my original 64 page booklet.

So I made him an offer. Play some more holdem using the stuff I had taught him and see how he does. If he was successful, he could then write a book using the notes he had taken as an outline. Then run it by me. We would be coauthors. He agreed and the rest is history. We titled the book Holdem For Advanced Players over Mason's objections. He was worried that players not in the advanced category wouldn't buy it. Because unlike me, Mason had not spent the previous dozen or so years seeing how people overestimated themselves. He acquiesced to my title request and the sales are now well over a quarter of a million like my two previous books. But this time there was no publisher to take most of the profits. We self-published. (And he quit his job) A year or two later we pretty much did the same thing all over again This time with Seven Card Stud For Advanced Players (with a bit of help from Ray Zee). At that point I suggested that Mason take over my original two books as well. Become a legitimate company. He did and named that company Two Plus Two Publishing. Other books were added, some written by Mason himself. Three were compilations of articles I had written elsewhere (including Getting the Best of It, required reading at Susquehanna). Followed by my books on Tournaments and No Limit Holdem. Later came excellent books by others especially Dan Harrington and Matthew Janda. Plus of course the twoplustwo.com website.

By about 1990 Mason was paying me enough to keep me from ever having to play poker or scheme again. But of course, I did anyway

Chapter Thirty-two: Three Creative (But Mean) Ideas For Bob

When I returned from LA at Bob's behest, he put me in a large suite where I was to remain for several years. In return for that, free food, and a nice salary, he got to scheme with me, usually during our many lunches together. I also got to sit in on almost any meeting he happened to be having if I was around. (One notable exception: I couldn't find Bob so I wandered into his small gourmet restaurant looking for him even though it was not yet open at that hour. He sometimes conducted meetings there rather than in his booth in the coffee shop. He was there alright. Sitting with Senator Harry Reid and Senator Richard Bryan! Both of Nevada's senators at the time. Two men I would have expected to be in Washington DC or Carson City were instead huddled with the "Polish Maverick" in his little restaurant. He later told me that they were simply asking for money. But who really knows?) For a while he even made me "Director of Operations". But that was abandoned when the Nevada Gaming Commission insisted I go through licensing procedures which, for various reason, I was not about to do. So I remained merely Resident Wizard and still spent most of my time playing poker and occasionally popping out a book.

Among the many schemes hatched in that coffee shop (or sometimes while the two of us walked through our or a competitor's casinos) were three I thought of that were highly profitable and outside the box. But they weren't very nice. Because they took advantage of the ignorance of average people. I love scheming when the people I am outwitting are simultaneously trying to outwit me. But when they aren't, it's a different story. And in these three cases I was not dealing with casinos or foes. I was merely trying to earn my keep and provide a financial cushion for a man who, as you will find out a little later, was not doing anywhere near as well as people thought. But in spite of being a little ashamed of these schemes, I am going to repeat them here because they also provide some good examples of creative thinking.

(What follows was also detailed in my book DUCY.)

1.   When people showed up at Vegas World via our Vacation Package, they were given a variety of perks, the main one being "one time use" chips with a total denomination of "$600" that had to be bet on even money propositions like blackjack or red or black on roulette. The chip was taken even if you won your bet. Thus, the EV of those chips was really only about $290. These chips brought the people to the table and they often continued to gamble once they were depleted. But some guests merely bet half their chips on red and half on black for the same spin, while betting about eight real dollars each on zero and double zero. They would walk away with about $285 and go about their business.

But it occurred to me that some of our guests might be both extremely risk averse and also not astute enough to see that they could guarantee themselves about $285 if they wanted to, or alternatively get close to that if they chose to spend a few hours at our tables playing normally. And that those people might instead be satisfied with two hundred dollars cash. Especially if the cash was what we originally put in their hands. So I suggested to Bob that when the guests checked in, the package not contain chips, but rather two crisp one hundred dollar bills with a note that said "please bring these two bills to our casino cage to obtain your chips." Bob resisted at first, thinking that no one would keep the money. But he decided to try it. Thirty percent of the guests kept the bills. And gave Bob about an extra quarter of a million dollars a month.

2.   We had a yearlong free slot tournament involving tens of thousands of entrants that was now down to four people who were about to go on the stage to play the final half hour round. The prize structure was very skewed. One million for first. $50,000 for second, $20,000 for third, and $10,000 for fourth. These were just average people who normally could only afford a budget style Las Vegas vacation. So it occurred to me that just like those people who took the $200 in scenario number 1 above, they might be very risk averse and ignorant of gambling theory and susceptible to a deal very favorable to Bob. Especially because the EV of each contestant ($270,000) was far above the second place prize. Was there any chance that they would all take a very ungenerous fixed amount rather than gamble? Again, Bob doubted it. But just in case he brought them all into a room and decided to see what would happen if he offered each of them the ridiculously low number of $60,000. Ridiculously low but still more than all but one of them would get if they played it out. They all accepted.

(Note: Bob chickened out the last second when our attorney, Andy Blumen, told him there was a good chance that the winner on the stage [which would have been merely theatrical had the deal been signed] would sue for $940,000. Almost certainly bad advice. My idea would save Bob $840,000 if Andy was wrong [or a bit less if he had to pay court costs to win a suit] and it would cost him a bit over 100K extra if Andy was right. Very good pot odds. Bob regretted his decision the next day.)

3.   Part of the Vacation Package sometimes included a free meal. (It also included a free show. That show was usually a pretty much over the hill entertainer who we could get for under 10 K a week; Robert Goulet, Jerry Lee Lewis, Debbie Reynolds, etc. Those entertainers did not

know the show was free and were thrilled when the showroom was "sold out." Just another little small deception going on at Vegas World.) Due to the nature of our ever expanding number of guests it was critical that we add a restaurant. But we had no place to put it. Bob and I walked through the place trying to figure out what to do. He showed me a smallish room that could accommodate about twenty tables but there was no place for a kitchen. And something hit my not exactly normal brain. The room had an exit that brought you out to the back of the building onto a very seedy street into a part of Vegas that was called Naked City. And a half a block down the road was a little Chinese takeout joint.

Could it possibly be legal to make that our "kitchen." Both Bob and I doubted it. But somehow Bob got the city's permission. So we built a lovely little "Chinese Restaurant" with flowers in vases and nicely dressed waiters. And when they took your order they retired into a tiny room with a phone, called the order into the takeout joint down the street, and waited for it to be wheeled up to the back door that was now, of course, hidden from view.

Chapter Thirty-three: Second Wife, Second Gun Pointed at Me.

This is not a long chapter only because I am not writing an autobiography. Robin Evans has been in and out of my life for many years. A couple of them married to me. Some of you may have met her when she lived in Las Vegas. Others, more recently, not knowing who she was, had some lengthy conversations with her on twoplustwo,com. Those who met her probably remember a very smart, pretty, and tempestuous individual and an excellent poker player. There were some not so wonderful things about her that I will mention as well. However, they pale in comparison to at least one good thing about her. She saved dozens of lives that otherwise would not have been saved. Actually, as a Las Vegas paramedic she saved hundreds of lives. I don't count all of them because most would have been saved by someone else had she not been the one sent to help them. But a few dozen would not. In some cases merely the fact that she was insanely good at what she did made the difference. But in other cases it went beyond that. She, in rare cases, disobeyed the rules, and risked getting fired, or even prosecuted. Because she knew the patient would probably die if she didn't. She was never wrong. So she was never punished for disregarding protocol (which usually meant giving higher doses of something than was technically allowed.) People are alive now because of Robin's courage and knowledge of both medicine and gambling theory

But her work for Mercy ambulance occurred years after we were together. We met in 1981 when she was dealing poker at Vegas World. She came up to me and asked me to explain something I had briefly talked about with a friend of hers. The idea that probability and the Gambler's Ruin Problem might be connected to certain unsolved number theory problems. Few pretty blondes had ever spoken to me at that point in my life and when they did Fermat or Goldbach conjectures were not their conversation openers. So I was immediately intrigued. More so yet when she actually seemed interested in the subject. Sherry was still in the picture, so at first we were just friends. She told me of a rough past in Georgia. She was an honor student but had an abusive mother and a father she never met. So she ran away from home. And met a much older notorious man who took her under his wing. Which included teaching her all the ropes of high stakes cheating in private games in the South. That's how she knew about an incident, described in the next chapter, involving someone who would go on to be one of the world's most successful gamblers.

After a few years she split up with her mentor and made her way to Vegas. After meeting me and accepting some poker tutoring, she quit her job and became a professional seven card stud player for a while. Few were better than her at 15-30 stud against the tourists in Caesar's Palace's poker room. Except perhaps when she was losing. She didn't go on full blown tilt but she did have an awful temper. Which was to show itself in all its glory a few years later. We had gotten married too soon after Sherry died. Indirectly that caused fights as Robin was to catch glimpses of my sadness. In the midst of one of those fights I got up and left the apartment. But when I got to the parking lot, I hear Robin behind me. I turn around and she is pointing a gun at my head. She forces me to walk back into the apartment. We sit down across from each other with the gun still pointing at me and she starts talking nicely. Then she gives me the gun! It did not have the desired reaction. I ran out a second time. Many people have been happy to have their life in Robin's hands. But me not so much.

Chapter Thirty-four: HI Stakes Dishonesty

By 1990, the cheating exploits of others no longer interested me much. My books, my patents, consulting and teaching, along with my scheming with Stupak was taking up more and more of my time and the poker world was fading into the background, except during tournament time. Yet ironically, I was hearing more and more about the dishonesty of folks, especially those in the upper strata of gambling. And not just from Mark. There were a couple of other people who were offering corroboration.

I don't think I should name names if the information is second hand. Or if it is someone you never heard of. That really only leaves one person who I will mention shortly. But will tell you about several things that were told to me that I have no reason to disbelieve. Some of you will have a pretty good idea about who I am talking about. But I will never go into more detail than what you read here (unless you break into my safe deposit boxes). I want my son to inherit a lot of money. But not until he is about 85.

I mentioned earlier that the very best cheaters plied their trade out of town and probably rarely cheated when playing poker in Vegas. I am thinking of people who you probably don't know. Al, Jimmy, and Jack being three of the main ones. Three guys who were not good enough to beat high stakes Vegas games "on the square". But even some world champions supposedly sometimes cheated. The most notorious one of course being the guy who knew everyone's hole cards on an internet poker site. But there is also the less well known champ who supposedly was his confederate in that scheme. Then there was the very well known WSOP championship winner who won that title because "Jimmy" was standing on the rail and signaling the hole cards of his opponents. Supposedly. (Bet you didn't realize I knew about that, did you buddy?) Then there were the two very high stakes gamblers who almost everyone assumed were honest gamblers. Perhaps because they both have had some voluntary interactions with the government which cheaters rarely do. In one case I already knew about his dishonesty before Mark told me because of a crazy coincidence. My ex-wife Robin knew a guy named Glen who had cheated with him via the installation of a "peep" in a bar in a southern state. Mark's information was an explanation of his dishonest giant score at a casino game that usually has no skill. The other guy Mark outed to me mainly played poker and bet sports but Mark told me that he was also making money using a "juice board" playing backgammon (plus doing other stuff in poker). A multiple bracelet winner. The first guy actually knows that I know about him. The second guy probably doesn't until he reads these words.

At least half a dozen of the people in the Poker Hall of Fame are over 90 percent in my opinion, to be cheaters. Another half a dozen at least, are completely undeserving due to incompetence. That's why when I was approached by people who asked if I had any objection to being inducted, I surprised them by saying "yes" (so they pursued it no further). Knowing what I know it was not an "honor" that my father would be proud of.

The cheater I will name is Chip Reese. Actually, he has publicly admitted it. But to my knowledge he somewhat downplayed it, saying something along the lines of he had to do certain things to be allowed to play the big games without being cheated himself. But it went further than that. I know this for a fact. I was privy to a couple of conversations between him and Mark that made his willingness to cheat clear. And these conversations were approximately during the same time that Chip was cardroom manager of the Dunes. The Dunes cardroom was crooked years earlier, but according to Mark it was worse yet when Chip was in charge. Cold decks, marked cards, etc. Also Chip almost certainly had help. The fellow who worked under him who somehow managed to avoid being tainted. Another name you probably don't know so I'll leave some doubt as to who he is.

111

I wish I could name the famous players of the past who were almost certainly not cheaters. I can't, aside from (supposedly)Eric Drachebecause I'm not that sure. Even Eric once took half of my action when I told him I could spot a blackjack dealer's hole cards. Legal but dubious. Another well known "honest" seven card stud expert got pumped up using an illegal method of manipulating slot machine handles. So you never know. On the other hand, I don't actually think most of the old time high stakes players were cheaters (except for the technically wrong practice of taking pieces of each other in big games.) And I have absolute no detrimental information about any player who was born after about 1960. Of course, most of these younger guys have college degrees and the ability to get high paying jobs, which was not the case for old timers. Chip himself almost certainly gave up dishonesty after he became adept at sweettalking rich amateurs into his game as well getting lucky in finding a brilliant computer programmer who could simulate baseball games and come up with more accurate odds than the bookies. I'm a little irked that he is considered the greatest all around player of all time as that is almost certainly an exaggeration. But not nearly as inaccurate as a lot of other generally accepted thoughts about those years.

Chapter Thirty-five: Lyle Berman Enters the Picture

Lyle Berman is in the Poker Hall of Fame but is definitely NOT one of those I was talking about with a cheating past or incompetent skills. But he is one of those I was referring to when I spoke of Chip Reese sweettalking wealthy amateurs into his game. Except that unlike those other amateurs, Lyle, in spite of being an "amateur", in the sense of not playing poker for a living, quickly became very good in a variety of different games. And for a while, possibly the very best at one game.

Lyle's business acumen eventually made him worth hundreds of millions of dollars. He owned some leather coat stores in Minneapolis, sold them, bought them back and did a lot of other business deals before I ever met him. Those who are interested can read his autobiography written with Marvin Karlins to learn the details. Later on, he got involved in the gambling business in a variety of ways and I played a part in some of them. It started out with his interest in poker. He made frequent visits to Vegas to indulge his hobby. And being a smart guy, he of course read my books. So even though I didn't play in the very big games he did (where I am almost sure he was sometimes cheated) he sought me out to discuss poker strategy

And he did more than discuss. A new game had recently hit the high stakes poker world. Pot Limit Omaha. And few, if any, players were all that good at it. Meanwhile, even though it was thirty years ago, Lyle had access to rather powerful computers for that time, that could spit out important info about the game. Occasionally Lyle would call me to discuss his computer results. But I don't think his opponents were aware of what he was doing. Almost certainly there was a period of time that Lyle knew more about pot limit Omaha than anyone in the world. That doesn't mean that he had to be the best player since the game requires more than knowledge. But as I said, there was a good chance he was.

A few years after I met Lyle, Native Americans were given the right to open casinos. One of the first places that was prepared to start were some tribes in Minnesota. But they had neither the money nor the expertise to build and run a major casino. They knew of Lyle and proposed a deal where he would put up the money and manage the place or places. Again you can find more details in his book. He did very well with them and shortly thereafter expanded his business, Grand Casinos, into Mississippi and Louisiana.

It occurred to me that the experience I had gotten at Vegas World could be used to help Lyle avoid mistakes, come up with profitable promotions, and improve his casino in other ways. And since I would be dealing with the person at the very top, I would avoid the aggravations of dealing with someone who would worry that the boss might say to him why didn't YOU think of that?" I wasn't looking for a full time job but I did like the idea of going out of town for a week and being sort of a "secret shopper" for the Grand Casino properties. Lyle agreed to my deal (and wasn't deterred when I warned him that I expected that 70 percent of my suggestions would not wind up working but pot odds made them worth trying) and I made three trips over the next couple of years. The only uncomfortable part of those trips would come at the end of my visit when I had to endure the hateful stares of the casino managers as they joined me and Lyle in a meeting where I enumerated my ideas and concerns. (I won't go into them here except to mention my favorite. In those days slot machines still took in and dispensed coins rather than tickets. Several times I would play one of the Grand's machines for various reasons. The third time I cashed in at the (now defunct) change booths for an amount between $50 and $100, I couldn't help but notice that the ladies in the booth kept giving me a fifty dollar bill. When I asked why, I was told. "The customers like that because when they get a fifty, they don't break it and put it back in the machine." When I relayed that conversation to Lyle and the casino manager you can imagine the reaction. Lyle proclaimed that one thing paid my salary for all the trips combined.

I will have more to say about Lyle and me shortly.

Chapter Thirty-six: Six More Thoughts

1. Venues that have very slow times such as movie theatres, bowling alleys, and perhaps amusement parks, should offer very steep discounts during those times, to those who have some sort of documentation that they would almost certainly never be able to afford regular prices or even typical discounts. Any business that does not incur much extra expense when customer numbers increase should consider this. There should still be a small fee, perhaps 15 or 20 percent of normal, to prevent overcrowding to the point where it would turn off ineligible regular customers (who are probably also being given a smaller discount during these times.)

2. Although I can't prove it, I believe that willpower can be improved through "exercise". At least for some people, including me. (I considered this idea so important that when if I first wrote a short chapter about it for my book Poker Gaming and Life, I put it in two different places! Both the Poker and Gaming Section and the Life section. I am unaware of any other book that repeats a chapter. [The later editions don't do this due to Mason being less of a fan of unconventionality than me.] The idea is to make the keeping of a promise to yourself more important than the subject matter of the promise. In other words, you make yourself immune to a rationalization that you should ignore your resolution, because of an excuse that you deem "logical".

    The great amateur poker player and successful businessman, Jay Heimowitz, said something to me during a World Series of Poker many years ago that made me start thinking about this stuff. He had been playing at Binion's for several days before the 10K main event.

He had done well at that event during previous years so I asked him whether he would play this year. To my surprise he said "no". He said that he only plays in the "big one" if he is up money at that point. And up to that point he was losing. I asked him if he realized that the field looked like it would be easier than usual. His reply was that he wouldn't change his mind in spite of this new unexpected information because he didn't want to "lie to himself".

I do think that idea can be taken too far. And in fact, I'm sure if there were a bunch of billionaire sultans entering the tournament the last minute, Jay would have changed his mind. But I do think that barring extreme circumstances, a good way to increase your willpower is to take pride in your ability to stick to resolutions INCLUDING resolutions that appear to have become dumb. And I think one way to do this is to give yourself trivial will power exercises. My favorite technique used video games and food. If I didn't score 50,000 on Missile Command, I had to order a Chef's Salad. Stuff like that. If you like Chef's Salad, you can think of your own

3. The difference in punishment between the crimes of murder and attempted murder should shrink. Same with drunk driving manslaughter and simple drunk driving. Or owning a building with lots of fire safety infractions compared to owning it when a fire kills someone. Why should luck make such a difference in what happens to that person? I'm sure you can think of many other examples.

4. If two unusual events may or may not be connected, and experts had proclaimed *before* the parlay occurred, that they are unlikely to be connected, you can now probably bet against the expert's original opinion. For instance, when they said that below freezing temperatures was

very unlikely to affect a Shuttle launch, you could assume that they could easily be wrong after the disaster. (They were.) When the Flipper, a man who could call coin flips because he somehow could slow down a twirling coin in his mind, divulged that he had Tourette's syndrome, I became almost sure that there was a connection even though I don't believe it was part of the medical literature. I've written about this before and the idea can be made more mathematically rigorous. In fact, Stanford statistics professor Persi Diaconis told me he started teaching the concept after he read what I had written. On the other hand, cops have known this stuff from before the time I was born.

5.   Sometimes released convicts who have spent many years in jail can't handle their new found freedom. So they commit a crime to go back. Obviously, it would be nice if we could identify those poor guys who feel like they have to do that and give them the help they need. But if we have failed it is ridiculous to simply wait and see what illegal act he may do, especially because someone may get hurt. Why not let him simply "stipulate" that he robbed a store or punched someone in the nose or whatever?

6.   If there is a statistical reason to "profile" a group of people for the supposed benefit of people in general, there is a simple criteria that would go a long way to helping the government decide whether to do it even if it is difficult to weigh the pros and cons. Would most members of the group be in favor of such profiling?

Chapter Thirty-seven: Electing a Senator / Challenging a Future President

Bob had just gotten a bunch of publicity by winning a million dollar bet on the Bengals in the 1989 Super Bowl. A short time after that, he was itching to come up with another stunt and he asked me if I had any ideas. I thought for a moment and came up with one. Donald Trump had just come out with a board game called Trump the Game. And he had advertised it a bit obnoxiously (no really, he did.) At the end of his ad he proclaimed something along the lines of "This game will show you whether you have what it takes or not. But if you don't, its OK. Just go home and enjoy the wife and kids". I told Bob to challenge Trump to play his own game for a million dollar bet. Bob replied that he had no idea how to play. I said "So what? He will almost certainly turn you down. But if he doesn't there is no way that I couldn't quickly learn it and then teach you to be a big favorite against him." Bob went along, as he almost always did when I made suggestions.

Full page ads were put into three east coast newspapers including the New York Post. They offered the challenge and ended with words similar to. "But don't worry Donald. If you lose you can always go back to the wife and kids." Trump wiggled out of the challenge using the excuse that he didn't want someone piggybacking on his name. Most assumed the real reason was that he was afraid he would lose. But he could have avoided people thinking that. All he had to say was "This guy didn't even realize that the game requires a minimum of three players."

We wound up getting national publicity well worth the price of the ads.

About the same time Bob had started a weekly newspaper, The Las Vegas Bullet. I barely remember it except for the fact that I wrote a few guest columns in the space usually reserved for Bob. And that almost certainly I, and that newspaper, changed the future of Nevada and a woman who as of the writing, is a member of the United States House of Representatives. Her name is Dina Titus. And she became a state senator in Nevada rather than settling for being a professor at UNLV, because I convinced Bob to write a negative story about her incumbent opponent, Terry Tebbs. Even though a high powered attorney, Tom Pitaro, was trying to convince him (in my presence) to do the same as other Vegas media and ignore it. The story involved a stripper and I need not go into further detail. Because the only important aspect to this story was that if the story became known it would almost certainly change the results of the election. That in turn brought up the more general question whether media outlets have a right to squash a story that would possibly change election results just because they themselves don't think the story *should* change the result. After Titus won the election and it was generally conceded that the Bullet story made the difference, I wrote a guest column defending our decision. Basically saying that if you believe that there are people who base their vote on a candidate's hair color and you believe that it is important that everyone has the right to vote, than if you are a news organization that finds out one of them dyes their hair, it isn't ethical to withhold that info. (Of course, in this case the story was much less trivial.)

Chapter Thirty-eight: Four PhDs Who Actually Liked Me

1. **Bill Bertram: Phd in Physics. Chief engineer for International Games Technology.** And a very nice guy who played poker on the side. If he wasn't so nice, he might have found it harder to like me. Because I caught a serious error he made that could have conceivably cost him his job. He miscalculated the payoffs on a new poker machine that IGT was distributing around town. Double Draw. You drew twice. A simple jacks or better game that obviously paid less for the various hands compared to the single draw variety. Except for the Royal Flush. That still paid $1000 dollars if you bet five quarters. But when I examined the game it immediately seemed to me that the payoffs were too high. And I thought I knew why. Bill hadn't thought something through (and everyone else at the company was evidently too dumb to do anything other than slavishly accept his figures.) He somehow didn't realize that the strategy for the first draw should no longer be the strategy that maximized the EV for that draw when there was no second draw. The most obvious example was a small pair vs a three card draw to a Royal. You no longer go for the pair. The game paid back about 103 percent vs optimum play. To double check that my math was right I played it at Vegas World until I hit a Royal. It didn't take long. Then I told Bob who told me to call up IGT. I called Bill directly and he was of course mortified. I believe they recalled the machines that same day.

2. **Douglas Hofstadter: Pulitzer Prize Winner. Author of Godel, Escher, Bach.** I went to hear him speak at UNLV sometime in the 90's and afterward got a chance to tell him my idea about a possible connection between the Gambler's Ruin Problem and some unsolved number theory problems. (Basically, the same idea Robin asked me about). I wasn't sure he

was interested. But several weeks later I get a call from him advising me that he had been discussing my idea with a professor from the State University of New York who would shortly be visiting Vegas and wanted to meet me. Unfortunately I don't remember his name. When he showed up not much progress was made with my idea. But I did give him a tour of the casinos. He had never been in one. And as I had mentioned in a previous chapter, he could not understand how anyone could play those games.

3.   **Nesmith Ankeny: Head of the Math Department at MIT. Author of a poker book that used game theory concepts to play high draw poker.** While playing in the same game as me, Ankeny who had read my books, asked me why I had not pursued a mathematics education. I replied that I sometimes regretted it but that it was now too late for me as I was 35 years old and only had one year of college. He then shocked me by saying that he thought he could get me into MIT's math department graduate school, bypassing three years of undergraduate courses. He extrapolated the words of my books to the point that he thought that I was smart enough to pull that off. Especially if he could get a second person to give a positive opinion of me. He did. That person was

4.   **Persi Diaconis: Professor of Statistics at Stanford and Harvard. Macarthur Prize Winner, World Class Magician, Famous for determining that seven shuffles essentially randomizes a deck of cards, Famous for proving that slightly more than 30 percent of all numbers found in the real world start with a "1."** And, of course he was also a poker player. But a poker player I had never met. So he also was putting his faith in his assessment of the words in my book. Later on, I did meet him in person when he joined the team at

Shufflemaster. That's when he told me that he had added to his lessons an idea of mine explained elsewhere that used math to help determine whether two events that occurred near the same time could be considered coincidences or not.

It goes without saying that I wound up declining MIT's offer. I realized that that I really wasn't interested in subjects that 99% would not really appreciate expertise in. Marilyn and Albert notwithstanding.

Chapter 39: Jackie Gaughan Bets Bob Stupak A Million On Mayor's Race

In 1987 the mayor of Las Vegas was a largely ceremonial position. But Bob Stupak wanted it. A lot. He had previously dabbled in politics but for this election he decided to pull out all stops. TV ads, professional election consultants, and stunts of dubious legality (like giant giveaways to voters who came to his casino). What he didn't do was grant interviews or give speeches. Because he knew almost nothing about how the city government worked or the issues it was dealing with. He was facing three opponents in the primary and if no one got over 50 percent, the top two would run off. He won the primary pretty easily and had to face Ron Lurie in the final.

During the campaign I had been urging Bob to familiarize himself with the issues because, with my help, he could actually be an excellent mayor. He partially relented and enlisted city councilman Steve Miller to have a lengthy meeting with me where we went over the relevant issues and aspects of the job after which I was to give Bob the Cliffs Notes. He was a decent student but never really showed much enthusiasm for the work of a mayor. The main thing was the publicity that being mayor would garner him. That and something else. He had bet iconic casino owner Jackie Gaughan that he would win. It was a private bet so I'm not sure if those two were committing a federal offense or not. In any case I have previously mentioned that this book would not name miscreants who I knew about second hand. And I am not breaking that pledge in this case. Because it was yours truly that walked into Mr Gaughn's office and handed him a briefcase containing 10,000 hundred dollar bills.

Chapter 40: Lyle Berman Creates "Sklansky Games"

I have invented several casino table games and as of this writing have patented two of them (as well as some patents involving slots and poker machines). Lyle Berman and his son Brad liked them well enough to give me a nice offer to own two thirds of the rights to the revenue from those games. We became equal partners in a company they formed and named Sklansky Games. The games, both based on holdem, were mildly successful. But they both suffered from the problem of dealer mistakes. Because it is not always that easy to determine the winner. Hopefully the games will be improved with technology so as to avoid that problem. In any case I want to briefly describe them because there were some interesting concepts associated with them.

One of them was easy for me to come up with because it had similarities to the game that I invented that I called Casino Poker and then turned into Caribbean Stud. But it was both more complicated and more interesting. We named it World Poker Tour All In Holdem. Just like Casino Poker the player makes an "ante" bet and then after seeing his cards, he either folds or bets more. The dealer "calls" when his hand is good enough to "qualify". But there are differences. Number one is that the decision as to whether to bet or fold (or call) is made after seeing only the player's (or dealer's) two card starting hand. Therefore, if there is a bet and a call the result is no longer instantaneous. The five board cards are dealt to determine the winner. Which means that a "bluff" with a poor hand is actually a "semi bluff" because it can win even if it is called. On the other hand, great cards are sometimes outdrawn. Also, in the original version the player had a choice of two different size bets- either five or ten times the ante.

There were two different calling criteria for the dealer. But unlike Casino Poker, those criteria were rather far from perfect GTO. Instead we opted for simplicity. Thus, the dealer called a

10X bet if her hand was "17" or higher and called a 5X bet if it was "13" or higher. Both those numbers were blackjack style. In other words J5 and K5 are both considered "15" (Aces are always 11). If there are several players at the table and some bet 5X while others bet 10X, a dealer who has a total of 14 will immediately pay only the ante to the larger bettors and deal the board out to determine the winner for the other bettors.

What I loved about this game is that the correct strategy is far from obvious. It is not simply fold bad hands, bet 5X with good hands and bet 10X with great hands. The perfect strategy requires a computer analysis. But in general, it is bet 10X with great hands and fairly bad hands, bet 5X with medium hands, and fold garbage. Bet ten with AA and 22, five with 88 and fold 72 offsuit. Those of you who are serious holdem players might want to see if you can figure out why. (The house edge against perfect play is tiny.)

The other game actually came first. Holdem Challenge. And unlike most of the other games I have invented, I don't remember what made me think of it. Perhaps it had something to do with my knowledge of how multiway pot poker is sometimes counterintuitive. In any case the game was simple. Deal out three face up two card holdem starting hands. Pick the one you think will do the best after the board is dealt. (Pushes that aren't beaten by the third hand are deemed break even.) Get paid even money. Obviously your chances of picking the hand that will wind up winning depends on what the three randomly dealt staring hands actually are. If they are AA, 22, and 22 or QQ, Q6 and Q3 you are well over 90 percent. On the other hand you are barely over 33 percent if the hands are something like 55, J6, and K3 suited.

So the question was what are your average chances? When I thought of the game I didn't know for sure. But I did know that in order for it to be a viable game I needed people to think it was slightly above 50 percent when in fact it was slightly below. Which was exactly the case. The winning chances averaged to about 47 percent (when someone picked perfectly). And when I went around the poker room and surveyed both high and low stakes players with this hypothetical question, most of their guesses were about 53 percent. Perfect. Except for the fact already noted, that in real life most casinos were paying off about 51 percent because the players said nothing when they were paid in error, but not otherwise.

NOTE: Both of the patents on the above games includes variations that have not yet been offered. Games besides holdem. Different bet sizes. More than three hands dealt. A second bet after the flop. Surrender. So if you are a casino or slot machine company owner you will probably have to go through me if you are interested in those variations or one of the several other games I have come up with.

Chapter 41: Ideas that Could be Wrong

I don't want to go so far as to call them "opinions". Opinions are often wrong. I consider these ideas 90 percent shots.

1. Poker is at least as likely as crossword puzzles and other games to prevent or slow down Alzheimer's disease. Furthermore, I think that some casinos, poker rooms and internet sites have lists that go way back that could help verify that claim. Anecdotally Doyle Brunson told me that of all the old-time players, he only knows of one who came down with the disease. I know of none. If I am proved right and internet sites offered low stakes games to players 50 and over, hopefully at a reduced rake, their business would skyrocket.

2. The reason why there is not as much pushback in the US to income disparity as might be expected is because cheap stuff has become so good. If you had unlimited access to everything at Walmart or even the better dollar stores (but could shop nowhere else) and had to drive a three year old Honda Civic, your lifestyle would, for the most part, exceed those of millionaires living in the 1970s. When people pay ten times as much, they usually get stuff not even twice as good.

3. Businesses should be allowed to buy out of the Disabilities Act regulations. Ramps, restroom accommodations, etc. But only if that money is mainly allotted for the disabled. How is that not win-win? If your business does not get a lot of disabled customers and you can donate half or so of what your cost would be to renovate, everybody gains except ramp makers.

128

4.   As sports betting becomes completely legal throughout the United States, there needs to be rules regarding the last few minutes of those games where the winner is clear but the pointspread wagers are still in doubt. Rules for things like last minute field goals. You are up by 16 as a 17 or 18 point favorite, and you have a fourth and goal with ten seconds left. The coach should not have it in his power to decide who covers. There should be a standardized accepted practice in such situations.

5.   Not enough kids are "left back". And those that should be but aren't, are practically doomed as they fall further and further behind as the years go by. Schools are very reluctant to do this because of the stigma involved. But I don't think that is a good enough reason. Furthermore, if a lot more kids do in fact get left back, the stigma would decrease.

6.   There are people who get ridiculously lucky when it comes to their jobs. Pro athletes, newscasters, singers, etc. People who if they weren't doing that job (or if the public lost interest in the job they had) would not have an alternative that paid anywhere near as much. Or to put it another way, people who wouldn't quit even if their salary was greatly slashed. I think those jobs should have an added tax tacked on above and beyond their normal tax rate.

7.   Cheating on your spouse behind his or her back is a bigger sin than some people make it out to be. Unless of course he or she has given you permission. Because he or she might have left you if he or she knew the truth. You may have deprived him or her from having a different

future from that he or she would have had if he or she found out what you did.

Chapter 42: A few More Stupak Stories

The first three I have written about previously. Not the last one though.

1.   Bob did not like to be threatened. And he liked to call bluffs. Both the Nevada Power

Company and the city government were to find that out. The power company was insisting

on a deposit even though Bob had been paying his bills on time. The government was

insisting that Bob comply with the law, and therefore plant more shrubs in front of his hotel.

The power company told him they would cut off all power if he didn't do it. The government

told him they would close the place down if he didn't do it. These two events happened at

different times. But in both cases his reply was basically the same. He wrote back something

along the lines of "Nope I'm not doing it. I look forward to seeing the newspaper headline:

400 Employees Out Of A Job at Vegas World. Not Enough Shrubs (Or No Electric Bill

Deposit). Needless to say, they both (I'm told) backed down.

2.   Vegas World was initially a small hotel. But the nature of his Vacation Club packages (as

will be explained soon) required us to expand. So Bob built a 20 story addition with about 22

rooms on each floor. When construction was nearly complete, Bob and I toured the place. On

each floor there was, in addition to the regular rooms, a small room perhaps 12 by 12 feet.

We guessed that it was designed to be used for maid's equipment. Bob lamented that if it was

50 percent bigger, we could have had twenty more rooms. But combining my knowledge of

circles and human nature I realized something that Bob hadn't. Put a mirror on the ceiling, a

circular bed under it, and gussy up the room in a few other naughty ways, and we would have

131

ourselves a tiny cramped room that some people would not at all complain about. And we did exactly that.

3.   The fact that our hotel was several blocks from the major strip hotels and even further from the Downtown ones would normally be a disadvantage. But because our Vacation Package filled up the hotel that fact became an advantage. If they were easy walking distance our guests would usually quickly leave us for them. And many of them did anyway. Thus I needed to think of a way to reduce that outflow. What concept could I use? The one I thought of stemmed from two incidents from my past.

When I was playing poker in the Bicycle Club in Bell Gardens, California there was a statewide instant scratch off lottery ticket that cost a dollar and offered a possible prize as high as $10,000 dollars. There was a guy who would go to the various tables and sell tickets to the poker players who wanted them. (They cost a dollar but had an EV of only 50 cents.). I decided to conduct an experiment. When a player was about to scratch off the covering, I would stop him and offer to buy the ticket for $3. No one ever accepted! They could not stand the thought that they would sell it to me and I would proceed to complete the scratching and win a big prize right in front of them.

The second incident occurred at Circus Circus casino in Las Vegas. I was showing the place to a ladyfriend who had never been in a casino. As part of the tour I bought an eight spot keno ticket for 60 cents. Shortly thereafter we left the place to walk to the Stardust. When we got halfway there, I realized that I had forgotten to check whether my ticket was a winner. It could be worth as much as $25,000 dollars! I started to insist that we walk back

132

since in those days they gave you only a limited time to cash or the ticket became null and void. Then I stopped myself. And considered how much someone would have to pay me to drag myself and my girl all the way back to Circus Circus if the only reason I was doing it was for that possible payment. The answer was at least ten bucks. Meanwhile the ticket was worth, on average, 45 cents. So I turned back around.

With those stories in mind I thought up the idea that a good way to keep our customers from leaving was to give them a free keno ticket several times a day while making it a requirement that they cash it within fifteen minutes of the numbers being drawn and displayed. And to take advantage of the psychological concepts involved (and to diminish accounting headaches) the payoffs were weighted toward the high prizes. (Up to, I believe, 50 K). But how were we to accommodate hundreds of guests four times a day? That's a lot of ticket writing. After a little thought I realized that this problem could be solved by assigning ten specific keno numbers to each room. The guest registered in that room automatically had those (ten) numbers. That scheme not only solved the ticket writing problem but also insured that every single guest had a reason to hang around at 3, 6, 9, and midnight. And I did one more thing. Although big prizes were rarely given out, with over ten thousand opportunities a week, decent sized awards were hit fairly often. And in spite of the enticement to stay in the hotel to see if they had won, there were still many who left. Thus there were many who would have won a nice prize (of at least $100 and sometimes much more) had they only stayed. So in case they thought that they would never know if such a result had befallen them, I had a large bulletin board put up with the first name, room number, and the amount of unclaimed prize of all those who would have won had they not abandoned us.

4. In spite of getting to the 85th percentile as far as girls were concerned, I was no match for the experts. Of which Bob was one. He was frequently making fun of my ineptitude in that regard. He told me that he had slept with about 2000 different woman. Most before he became rich. (He also told me that he was far behind two other Vegans. Dr .Elias Ghanem [Elvis's doctor] and photography entrepreneur Morgan Cashman both of whom he claimed bedded 5000.) When I expressed a little skepticism while we were having a drink at the bar at his place, he decided to refute me by suggesting that I walk through the hotel and pick an unaccompanied female playing slot machines for him to shoot at. I chose a nice looking girl, perhaps 25 years old. But how was I to know for sure what degree of success Bob had? "You will be there the whole time" Bob replied. What? Unless this was a preplanned setup (I later knew for sure that it wasn't.) Bob was suggesting that he could accomplish a task with constraints that Don Juan himself shouldn't be able to overcome.

We walk over to the slot machine and Bob, after quickly introducing me, starts chatting with her. (He does get around to telling her he owns the place so in that one respect his demonstration is somewhat tainted, scientifically speaking.) I just sit there and say nothing (which was our agreement). After about twenty minutes Bob invites her to dinner at his nicer restaurant. The three of us in a booth. Again, I am practically wordless. After dinner he invites her to come up to her suite. She accepts and they go up the elevator. With me. At no point did Bob offer an explanation as to why I was still with them. We go into the suite, Bob offers her a drink and they talk a bit more. I'm still basically silent. Then they start doing it. Right in front of me. When they are done Bob quickly gets dressed and leaves. I'm still there. I don't know about you but I'm feeling a bit awkward. I make conversation by asking her about herself and determining that there seems to be nothing out of the ordinary about her past or her life. (I actually ran into her a few times after that and that opinion did not change.) We left shortly thereafter and I never uttered a word about it thinking no one would believe me. I hope you appreciate it that I have chosen you to be the one to whom I break my silence.

Chapter 43: Harvard Doctors Arrogantly Excuse Their Math/Logic Ignorance

Supposedly smart people constantly make a serious mistake regarding experiments, polling and clinical trials. Several years ago, the doctors who put out the Harvard Health Letter not only made this mistake but also, when called on it, compounded their sin by claiming that they should not be expected to be that adept at statistical inference. They wrote that, even though their error could be understood by an intelligent 12 year old and even though the error they made could be the cause of people dying.

I have written about this error before. And I am not the first one to do it. In fact it is probable that literally thousands have before me. Yet the error persists even in the minds of many of those who have graduated Harvard Medical school and are likely to be doing, or reading, studies where it is critical that this error not occur, but often does.

It's really very simple. If you suspect a gizmo, a coin, a drug or whatever is out of the ordinary, and when you use it multiple times and get out of the ordinary results, you still don't know how likely your suspicions are actually correct. Not if the merely ordinary gizmo, coin or drug sometimes gives you the exact same result when used multiple times. And especially not if your suspicions were originally considered farfetched. To think otherwise is the error I speak of.

Take the coin. You suspect it is weighted towards heads. Say you know that the government made a few that come up heads about 60 percent of the time. You proceed to flip it 100 times and get 60 heads. You know that a fair coin will come up heads 60 or more times out of a hundred flips, only about 3 percent of the time. What are the chances that you were flipping a weighted coin? Please don't say 97 percent. Please don't say that there is a 3 percent chance the coin is a fair one. If you did you could not be more wrong. Suppose for instance that the government made only 15 bad coins versus the millions made correctly. Do you really think that if you flipped a coin in your pocket and got 60 heads that it is probably (let alone 97 percent) one of the bad ones? It's not even one percent to be.

It is almost exactly the same thing if a drug (or a placebo) is known to cure a person half of the time. And a new experimental drug is given to 100 people and cures 60 of them. The likelihood that the new drug works better than the old one is related to how farfetched the underlying theory behind that drug's efficacy is. And in almost no case is it correct to think that there is a 97 percent chance that it actually works better. Yet it was exactly something along those lines that was written by Harvard doctors in the Harvard Health Letter about fifteen years ago. And when I wrote them a letter to point it out, they wrote back acknowledging their error. Fine. Except in their next addition they, without acknowledging what they wrote in their previous edition, started talking about how the subject of statistics can be confusing and how as doctors, they shouldn't be expected to know the ins and outs of the subject. Even, I guess, Statistics 101. Shame on them.

Chapter 44: Some Investing / Betting Concepts

1. My "Fundamental Theorem of Investing"

I coined that term quite a while ago as a way to label an idea that is pretty obvious but is rarely spelled out. Which is that before you make a major financial transaction that you think is plus EV, (whether it be buying or selling stock, betting on a football game, or any of a variety of transactions where individuals are taking the other side,) you ought to have a pretty good idea of why they are doing that given you think they are wrong. If you can't explain their willingness to take the other side in spite of the fact that (in your opinion) it is negative EV for them, you should seriously reconsider making that transaction. In other words, you need to identify why they have misevaluated the known information, or don't have the information you have, or possibly have tax or marginal utility reasons to make the deal. Otherwise you might be heading into a trap.

2. Paying For Information

Suppose there are two pennies in a hat and they are both biased. They look the same but one comes up heads 80 percent of the time while the other one comes up heads only 40 percent. You find a guy who doesn't know this and is willing to bet $100 on tails after a penny is drawn randomly. You are about to agree when another guy makes you an offer. With his special glasses he can tell you which coin has been picked with 90% accuracy. (But he will be wrong 10 percent regardless of the coin.) You are allowed to back out of the bet after the coin is picked. So up to how much can you pay this guy for his (slightly inaccurate) information?

If that second guy didn't show up your EV is $20. The simplest way to figure that is to consider that the coin will average showing up heads 60 percent which makes you $200 ahead after ten tries. Or you could say that after ten tries you will pick the good coin five times and get four heads and pick the bad coin five times and get two heads. Again a $20 EV. Now let's figure out the EV if we make a deal with Guy 2. First notice that the good coin when flipped provides you with a $60 EV. The bad coin costs you a $20 EV. If we make the deal 100 times, we will back out 45 times and erroneously bet 5 times. That will cost us an average of $100. We will bet on the good coin 45 times (not 50) making an EV of $60 each time. That's $2700. A net profit of $2600 after 100 times. $26 EV. So the fair value for the info was only the $6 it added to your EV. Didn't you think it would be more?

When evaluating the value of extra information, you must consider three things. How likely is it to be accurate? Even if it is correct, how likely is it that the information will change the decision you would have made if you didn't have it? Even if it is accurate and it changes your decision, how much do you gain from that change?

3. Passing up a good bet for a better one coming up shortly.

It is never right to do that if you can easily afford to make both bets. And even if you can't, it is almost always right to make the first bet if the second bet can now be much larger those times you won the first. Where it gets tricky is when there is a limit to the size of the allowed bets and you can't afford to make that second bet if you lose the first bet. It's tricky because it is not necessarily correct to say that you skip the first bet if the second one is better.

To illustrate, first consider the situation where you have a hundred dollars to risk and the two upcoming possible bets are 60 percent and then 2/3. If there is no limit and you want to maximize your EV, you simply bet the hundred on the first bet and, if you win, bet the whole $200 on the second bet. 40 percent of the time you will go home with $400 for an average of $160. If you had only made the second bet you would go home with $200 2/3s of the time. $133.33 Clearly you should make both bets. If you can only bet $100 on the second bet even if you win the first bet then if you bet both you will have $300, 40 percent, $100, 20 percent (win followed by loss) and zero 40 percent. That's $140 EV. Which is still better than waiting for the second bet. But what if the first bet is 60 percent and the second bet is 80 percent (and you can only bet $100 on the second bet)? Betting both leaves you with $300 48 percent, $100 12 percent and zero 40 percent. That's an EV of $156. While waiting is an EV of $160. So in this case you should wait

Finding the breakeven point is a simple algebra question. But even without algebra these examples should show you that in order to pass up a good bet for a better one later, you pretty much need a situation where a win of the first bet won't allow you to increase the bet on the second one AND that second bet is A LOT better than the first one.

4. Taking Advantage of Near Efficient Markets

Most experts agree that pointspreads, moneylines, and stock prices are almost always priced efficiently. In other words the results of major pro and college football and basketball games is that almost exactly half cover the spread and half don't (ignoring ties). Of all the baseball games that are

160-140 almost exactly 60 percent of the favorites win. If a stock is $50 today the EV of its price a year from now is about $53 (because stock prices average increasing about 6 percent a year). Put another way, the efficient market hypothesis basically asserts that the market essentially accurately assesses the multiple factors that goes into a stock price or a pointspread.

But if this theory is true, which for the most part it almost certainly is, it means that being knowledgeable about many factors is of little use. And that is easily verified if you follow sportswriters who are occasionally given a hypothetical bankroll to "bet" their picks in the newspapers or recommendations of brokerage houses or the experts on CNBC. They are on average rarely better than monkeys throwing darts.

But there is a silver lining to this. It means that if, for some reason, you have identified just one fairly important factor that is either little known or is being misevaluated, you need not worry that you are unfamiliar with most of the factors regarding a sports contest or buying or shorting a security. Almost always the factors you are not considering are being correctly evaluated. So you don't have to waste a lot of time studying all those "fundamentals" that the bean counters study, usually to no avail (Although sometimes the unusual misevaluated factor may indeed be something only astute bean counters will recognize.) Instead you can now check out a lot more possible bets until you discover an obscure fact like a quarterback who is more negatively affected than usual by cold weather or extra pretty cheerleaders.

Chapter 45: Some Interesting Short Stories

Some anecdotes from about the year 2000.

1. Bob and I fly to Wendover Nevada to check out the casinos there and perhaps buy one. Its my first flight on a small plane, which in this case was a six passenger Lear Jet with a pilot and a copilot. I wasn't looking forward to it because flying on a commercial airliner makes me nervous in spite of the left side of my brain knowing that you are 100 times or so more likely to die in a car going that same distance. Most likely it's because I am putting my life in other people's hands and I am not one to trust other people.

But I had no anxiety during the flight. And because of the way my mind works I had to know why. And I think I figured it out. It was probably because I could see out the cockpit window! I could theoretically alert the pilots if something was approaching. If my theory is correct it could perhaps be used to develop some sort of therapy to help those who are control freaks or have similar problems.

2. Bob had started dating Phyllis McGuire of the famous McGuire Sisters. But she was also famous for another reason. Being the girlfriend of big-time mobster Sam Giancana during the 60's. They went to great lengths at times to avoid the prying eyes of the press with varying degrees of success. In 1975 Sam was the victim of a hit. (I have no reason to think that Phyllis was in any way involved in Giancana's misdeeds.) Meanwhile she had moved into a mansion in Las Vegas where she met Bob. I have been inside her house several times including twice with my parents. Meanwhile I had become friendly with the poker shift manager at Vegas World. Benny. A guy who had escaped

Russia (actually Ukraine) while they were still communistic. Benny went on to become a great poker player and has a World Series of Poker bracelet.

One day Bob invited me to dinner at Michael's gourmet restaurant in Vegas. I happened to be with Benny at the time so I asked if he could come along. That was fine and Bob decided to invite Phyliss as well. During the dinner, Benny, who didn't really know much about Phyliss, was asked to give us some details about his escape. During which he turned to Phyliss and said "Do you have any idea what it feels like to travel many miles in the trunk of a car?" To which Phyliss replied "Of course I do." Bob and I had a good laugh at Benny's confusion before explaining the crazy coincidence. Not sure if there is a lesson to be learned from this but thought the story was cute enough to repeat regardless.

3. While sitting at a poker game the subject of batting averages came up. They were talking about averages before the All-Star break compared to averages afterward. This prompted me to make the observation that Player A could have a lower batting average than Player B in both the first half of the season and the second half yet still have a higher average for the full season. No one believed me. So I said I'd bet $100 that I could prove it in 30 seconds. High stakes player Billy Baxter who was playing smaller than usual, threw a $100 bill at me saying he expected to lose but it was worth it to hear the explanation. So I told him to imagine that player A goes 30 for 90 (.333) in the first half and one for 10 (.100) in the second half. Player B goes 20 for 50 in the first half (.400) and 10 for 50 (.200) in the second half. 310 vs 300. If you use this please send my commission care of Two Plus Two LLC in Las Vegas.

4. My buddy Eddie was bitter that he never had a chance to reach fame and fortune in the two fields where he had a lot of talent. Baseball and Impersonation (as in Frank Gorshin or Rich Little). He grew up near Joliet, Illinois which was home to several pro baseball players. And Eddie knew that every one of them had dads who spent several hours a week honing their son's skills. Eddie's dad did not. But Eddie's dad was not an athlete as the other dads were. Because of genetics it is almost certain that Eddie's natural ability was only excellent rather than world class. As far as his ability as an impersonator, an endeavor he practiced at quite a lot, I knew he was good but I wasn't sure how good. Eddie claimed he was good enough to make it professionally if he only had known the right people. Then one day while I was having dinner with him, Bob, who knew Eddie only from the poker world sat down to join us. I used the opportunity to bring up Eddie's talent and his gripe. Bob immediately offered Eddie a gig in his lounge! And Eddie turned it down. He was forced to admit the truth to himself that he almost certainly wasn't good enough. And the incident might have caused him to rethink his opinion of his chances to have made it in pro baseball as well.

The incident unsurprisingly made Eddie quite depressed. And it got me to thinking. Most of those people who complain that if not for their difficult circumstances (or their unwillingness to be "dishonest in business") they would have been a big success; may actually be lucky they have that excuse. Now they can go through life under the misapprehension that they would have otherwise made it. It is often said that it is better to have tried and failed than never to have tried at all. But I'm not so sure.

5. A very big (honest) game was going on in the Mirage. It had lasted several days with high rollers coming and going. Bobby Baldwin, now mainly a casino honcho, was no longer considered one of

the best players especially if the game was not no limit holdem. I think that bothered him. And very

likely he was being underestimated. On the other hand, being underestimated is an advantage. And

the money changing hands was large enough that Bobby was almost certainly more concerned with

keeping that advantage than helping his ego. But I provided him with an opportunity to do both.

Because of my books and my notoriety, I could be considered an equal even though the games I

played in were only about one tenth the size of this big game. So it wouldn't be beneath him to let me

in on a secret he knew I would keep (until now). About 40 hours after the game started, I walked

into the Mirage card room and after watching the game for a few minutes, Bobby walked up to me

and asked me to take a walk. We went up to his room. He opened up a drawer of the dresser. And

showed me about three hundred thousand dollars in chips which he had slowly taken off the table.

Chapter 46: National Gaming Impact Comission

With gambling proliferating, President Clinton formed a study commission to conduct hearings that travelled throughout the country. I was to be one of the witnesses when they reached Las Vegas. My job was to explain the details, including the house edge, of the various casino games. While I was waiting to testify, other witnesses were testifying about the harm casinos do to those who are compulsive gamblers. The casino representative who testified before me tried to defend casinos with words along the lines of "casinos do not count on their customers having a gambling problem". I started my testimony with words along the lines of "that's true but they do count on them being ignorant." As mentioned previously Terri Lanni , CEO of MGM, who was one of the nine members of the commission (that included three members from the casino industry) went on to agree with that assessment in a subsequent private conversation. And he also somewhat inappropriately interrupted my testimony to defend his properties after I was very critical of one particular bet offered on craps tables. The Big 6 and Big 8. Bet either one comes before a 7 and they pay you even money on something that occurs only 5 out of 11 times. That's a terrible bet. But it wasn't the main reason I was so opposed to it. Rather it was because you could make the exact same bet on a different spot on the layout and get 7 to 6 odds. 1.167 to 1 rather than 1 to 1 on a 1.20 to 1 shot. Much less bad. And only beginners would be both unaware of that better option and the terrible payoff of the first one. So I thought it was pretty disgusting that a casino would offer such a sucker bet that only beginners would take.

Apparently, the MGM properties had recently come to that same conclusion. They had removed the bet though others hadn't. And Lanni made sure to put that information into the record. I guess I can't blame him.

There were a few other noteworthy short conversations I had before my actual testimony. One was with Tom Grey who was a clergyman and a big-time crusader against gambling. We were chatting while I was waiting to testify whereupon he decided to confess to me that he enjoyed playing poker. He didn't really consider that gambling given the skill involved and the fact that unlike casino games, it was hard to lose far beyond what you originally budgeted. Of course, I agreed. He asked me not to tell anyone but I don't think anyone will care 20 years later. Another conversation occurred the day before. Evidently the bigwigs of the casino industry were very worried about my testimony. And they were perhaps right to be. It would have been easy for me to spin casino gambling into an anti social business similar to the cigarette business. But I had decided to go easy on them and instead simply highlight my erudition on the subject. Not knowing that, Gary Loveman CEO of Harrahs, called me with a request to summarize what I was planning to say. Since he had never chosen to speak to me until that moment I decided to make him sweat a little bit and I refused his request. Shortly thereafter Bobby Baldwin who was then running the Bellagio called. He had never called me before. He asked me a poker math question. Nothing else. I answered him and got off the phone

I wasn't sure how angry I should be. It was inconceivable that the call was really about a poker question. But what was his intention? Was he threatening retribution if he didn't like my testimony. That would have been totally unacceptable. Or was he simply trying to butter me up by complimenting my math skills and hoping that would influence me away from saying anything too bad the next day. The problem was that even this second option was unacceptable. This was a hearing commissioned by the PRESIDENT. My father was following it. A chapter back I was talking

147

about Bobby being approximately my "equal". But he was not my father's equal. Meshulem Riklus, owner of the Riviera Hotel/Casino in Las Vegas talked about how when he went to Israel to visit his world class physicist brother, he was considered a nobody compared to him. And they were right. There are thousands of people, many still alive, who know math or physics much better than they would have if they had just about any other teacher than my father.. No one in the casino business is remotely his equal. There is no way I would have altered my testimony one iota to please those people if I thought it would displease him.

Chapter 47: The "Vacation Club" Morphs Into a Pyramid Scheme

One day Bob and I were strolling through the Gaming Show in Vegas when we came to an auditorium that was about to present a lecture on casino marketing. I suggested we go to it. Bob poo pooed the idea saying that he already knew more than anyone else about the subject. I countered that if we learned just one thing it would be worth it. He relented. The place was full. 200 people. The teacher went to the lectern and started out by saying that he will be explaining several ideas. But for the most part all you really needed to understand was something he took out of his briefcase and showed to the audience. It was the mailer soliciting $400 for Bob's Vacation Club package. Bob feigned being angry at me for wasting money on the seminar. But I knew he was loving it.

The problem was that the teacher was wrong. The Vacation Club had become an unprofitable Ponzi scheme. And even at its height it was only mildly profitable. It kept the hotel at 100 percent occupancy but it was an optical illusion .

Furthermore, the VC was a semi scam. It advertised a great deal when the actual deal was only borderline OK.

Roughly speaking, the mailers and magazine ads for the VC asked for people to send in $400, and then visit the hotel anytime in the next two years or so. When they got there, they would supposedly pick up perks that were "worth over $1000". Actually, they were worth about $370 plus whatever value you placed on two or three nights in a mediocre hotel room. The ad said you were getting $600 in chips, $400 in slot play, and a diamond ring worth hundreds. The truth was that the chips were worth about $290 at most, the slot play was worth about $35 and the rings cost us $45 each.

The $30 profit to Vegas World was of course insufficient. Especially given the cost of all those mailings where fewer than 1 percent signed up. But then you add in the amount that the players lost in the casino. Which was a bit more than $100 on average. Partially due to the fact that the hotel was isolated so you couldn't just walk across the street to a nicer one.

98 percent of the guests in the hotel came from this package. Without it the occupancy would have probably been 25 percent rather than 100 percent. But more and more when guests showed up and used their pseudochips and slot play, the money they pocketed came from $400 payments from yet to arrive guests. At first the bottom line was that a guest paid $400, lost about $130 ($30 + $100), we got $400 and paid perhaps $80 on average to obtain a guest. So, we made $50 per guest minus the expense of running the place. At first.

But the problem was that as it got harder and more costly to sell a package it wasn't immediately obvious because it didn't hurt the operation in the short run. So Bob kept selling, not fully realizing that if things didn't turn around (which they would if a much higher percentage of customers bought the package or if somehow the average casino win increased dramatically, or, if he came up with a brilliant idea like the Stratosphere Tower) he was probably on his way to jail.

Chapter 48: A Trip To Russia Gives Us Ideas

It was becoming clearer and clearer that things at Vegas World could not continue on the path it was

going down. Customers were not buying the Vacation Club at the same rate they used to. To sell one

package required over a hundred dollars of expenditures. And there seemed to be no way to remedy

that. When a customer showed up, we had to come up with about $370. That couldn't be changed.

Nor could we increase the $400 price tag. We could temporarily stave off disaster by selling more

and more packages at a loss but we had two years at best before we would be unable to honor our

obligations to arriving customers. Our only hope would be to entice the guests to lose or spend more

than they had been, or to somehow entice people to come who weren't staying in the rooms (which

were at 100 percent occupancy due to the packages). Double Exposure, Crapless Craps, and Experto

21 were no longer the draws they once were when they were first introduced. I was racking my brain

trying to come up with yet another game that would fool customers into thinking that they had an

edge when they really didn't. But it seemed impossible, mainly because the public had caught on that

Bob, or someone who was advising him, was shrewd enough to not actually offer such a game.

Then one day I walk into the coffee shop that Bob used as his office, saw that he was looking at some

photographs and literature and seemed to be in a surprisingly good mood. When I asked him what

was going on he told me that he thinks we will be going into the observation tower business. What?

He tells me that he has discovered that every major observation tower in the world is very profitable.

There was a perfect spot next to the casino. And if we built a tower there, we would not only profit

from the tower itself but also, presumably, from the fact that visitors would sometimes stay and

gamble.

If Bob's information was correct it seemed like a good idea. Except of course that we didn't have anywhere near the money it would cost to build such a thing. But before worrying about that we thought we should check out a couple of towers and gather a bit more information. That first brought us to Seattle, a place that not only had a tower but also some well regarded engineers. Seattle's tower isn't that high but still it was doing well and we enjoyed the dinner in its revolving restaurant at the top. And the info we got from the engineers did nothing to dissuade our plans.

The second place Bob wanted to check out was somewhere I didn't even know had a tower. Moscow. I wasn't thrilled but I said OK. Bob, me, and three others arrived during the time Gorbachev was in charge but had not yet put in his reforms. We stayed at the Metropole Hotel where each of us had a $500 a night room. The best hotel in Russia, across from the famous Bolshoi Ballet. When we got there, Bob quickly wanted to check out the Russian woman and we found some advertisements from females who were hoping to marry an American. Legitimate ads, not hooker ads. I met a nice pretty lady named Marianna, and went out with her four times during the week I was there. The first time we met I took her to the Metropole Buffet. Her mind was blown. She made about $50 a week as a secretary and couldn't fathom a $20 buffet. Remember that Russia was still a poor, communistic, police state. Few people had cars. Almost all got around in their beautiful subways, including Marianna.

While choosing food at the buffet, Marianna got especially excited when we got to, of all things, the kiwi fruit. It was displayed nicely with cut up fruit in the middle of the tray with uncut fruits surrounding them. She said she that only one other time in her life had she tasted or even seen kiwis. I told her to take one home. But there was no way she would do that as there was a sign that said that they expected you to only avail yourself of food that you would completely eat at your table. We had a nice lunch and got to know each other. Then I walked her back to the subway station. When we got halfway there, I asked her to stop for a minute. I reached into my pocket and handed her four kiwis. I thought she was going to have a heart attack. I started laughing and tried to explain to her that as a member of a group that was spending a truly insane amount of money at their hotel, even the KGB would forgive my four kiwi theft. She was not really placated which I found quite interesting. But she did wind up taking the fruit.

Meanwhile while Bob and I were touring the town in a cab a day or two later, we were suddenly surrounded by three new Lincolns. Several well dressed men jumped out and I thought we might be about to be kidnapped. Instead they said that they were there to escort us everywhere we went and make sure we stayed safe. Which they did. Even though we never actually found out exactly who they were. Our best guess was that they were working for people who had recently been allowed to open casinos in Moscow and thought they might soon be doing business with Bob. Or maybe they were just Russian Mafia members who got wind of us and thought it would be bad publicity if any harm came to us.

On our second date Marianna and I went to one of those new Moscow casinos. While there we passed a table named Asian Poker. Make an ante bet and then back up your five card hand with another bet twice that, or fold and give up your ante. The dealer will call you with AK high or better. When I told her that they had stolen my game and changed the name, I decided not to pursue it when she looked at me like I was crazy.

Our third date was at Moscow's major art museum. A place that was free to all. She begged me to

153

accompany her because they were having a special exhibit of Salvidor Dali's art. Sure why not? Except when we got there the line was a quarter of a mile long. Literally. I was not a happy camper. Seeing my distress Mariana said "Well there is a way to get right in but it costs a lot of money". "How much", I asked. "Seven dollars each." Needless to say, we were inside the museum two minutes later. But the incident got me to thinking. Seven dollars was not at all insignificant to the average Russian. It was similar to what a hundred dollars would be to an American nowadays. Also, the high cost to avoid the line was not a secret program. Everyone knew about it. That sort of seemed odd in a communist country. Why was the program tolerated? My conclusion was that it was tolerated because the cost was so high. If it had been let's say two dollars the average Russian would still not have paid it but they would feel bad about it. At seven dollars they instead felt that those paying it were being ridiculous. But they were also helping the museum financially. Thus, if rich people want to be that silly why not let them?

I realized that these thoughts might be used to come up with some good ideas for Americans as well. I will mention a couple of them shortly.

Near the end of our trip we visited the Moscow tower and its surprisingly nice revolving restaurant at the top. When I say "we" I of course mean Bob, myself, Marianna, and a bunch of Russian mobsters. (I still have the photos to prove it) We left Moscow with Bob almost certain about the project that he hoped would let him escape what otherwise would be a sad fate.

Chapter 49: Soak the Rich. Where They Park

The incident at the Russian Art museum that charged visitors a big fee (by their standards) to avoid the line, brought back a memory. A story told to me by a buddy who hustled for a living and was enamored with high stakes gamblers. He told me of a time where two of them were playing gin rummy for big money while sitting by the pool at a major Vegas hotel. It ended with one of them owing the other $50,000. They apparently seriously disliked each other. Because when the loser was getting ready to pay, the winner announced, in front of all the bystanders, that he would forgive the debt if the other guy would jump into the pool with all his clothes on. And the other guy refused and paid!

I don't know how true this story is. But it doesn't matter because my reason for retelling it has to do with my buddy's take on it. He was expressing admiration for the guy who "refused to make a fool of himself for money" in front of all those people. But he was wrong. And I am almost sure you would agree. He was actually making a fool of himself by NOT jumping in. Maybe he would have deserved respect if he turned down $1000 or even $5000. But $50,000? C'mon. If this story is true, the bystanders probably thought the guy was an idiot. My friend didn't only because he romanticized the situation.

The point was the average person does not feel bad when a rich person foolishly spends far more than he or she would, for something they deem silly. And this is doubly true if some of that silly expenditure is returned to them in some way. For instance, if a row of seats at a movie theatre gave massages and the theatre charged $100 each for them while reducing the prices for other tickets by a dollar, very few people would be offended that the theatre was instituting a policy that "shamed" the

non rich. (Assuming the massages didn't distract others from the show) I highly doubt that this

particular scheme would get many takers. But I think a less ridiculous one would.

There is a raging debate going on as I write this book as to how high the ultra rich's taxes should be

or whether there should even be a "wealth tax". The debate won't end anytime soon. Because rich

people don't like the government taking and spending a high percentage of the money they have

made on things they don't agree should be bought. But their attitude would certainly be different if

the money that they were giving to the government was a trivial amount (to them) for something that

they want. Even if they are vastly overpaying by most people's standards. Bill Gates once wrote how

he gave a pizza shop about $300 to stay open ten minutes later than usual and bake a pizza. And why

shouldn't he?

It is totally understandable that people would be offended if rich people were given the opportunity

to pay moderately more than the average person could afford, for something critical. A medical

procedure or an expensive cancer drug for instance. Or a generator whose price was raised during a

hurricane. But I maintain that for something much less important it would be no big deal if rich

people were given the opportunity to seriously overpay, especially if some of that money comes back

to the less fortunate and doesn't inconvenience any else to a major extent. Pay $100 to ride the

carpool lane during non busy times without a passenger. Or any of a myriad of other things (some of

which are already being done, such as paying more to expedite a passport.) But my favorite example,

of which I have written about in the past, is more controversial even though it shouldn't be. Because

some people overemphasize some weak, mainly emotional, counter arguments.

Put very expensive parking meters on about half of the handicapped parking spots. Perhaps charge a dollar a minute. Let them pay with a credit card. The meter should be fitted with a gizmo such that it knows when you leave, charges you for the precise amount of time you are there and then resets to zero. Unless you want to take the option of paying extra. Or if you want to put money in the meter without even parking. You might do that because most of the money collected by these meters will be siphoned in some way back to those who actually need those handicapped spots.

When I have mentioned this idea to others, a few have protested that my idea would sometimes burden the handicapped driver. But it would be easy to keep that to a minimum. For instance, you could have the meters working only during non-busy or moderately busy times. Surely you have been in parking lots where lots of empty handicapped spaces are beckoning yet you have go to the trouble of finding a space elsewhere. Even if you aren't rich you might fork over a couple of bucks to make a quick trip inside a store. (I suspect that nowadays it would be no big deal for the number of paid spaces to change in real time depending on availability. Or to set up meters that can shut off if a handicapped person wants to use the space.) And if after all that there are still very occasionally times where a handicapped driver has to wait a minute or two, I would expect he would easily tolerate it given the benefits he gains from my idea.

The other objection I have heard is that people will be offended by the fact that they are "exposed" as people who can't afford to use the meter since they park elsewhere. I think I have given some pretty good reasons why you shouldn't buy that silly argument.

Chapter 50: Four More Short Stories

1. My last real big poker score. I came in 3rd at the World Poker Tour televised final event at the Borgata in Atlantic City. I picked up over $400,000 but my last hand was debatable. Got all in with a pair of fives getting only about 7-5 odds where my opponent probably had TT, JJ, QQ, AK, or AQ. Total combinations 6+6+6+16+16 = 50 Of those I should win about 1+1+1+9+9 =21. So its real borderline. What made my decision was the five days in a row I hadn't gotten enough sleep and the toll it was taking on me. I was no longer playing my best and was trying to get the tournament over quickly, one way or the other.

2. Some cars parked in the Vegas World garage were getting broken into. The garage had no security cameras because they were fairly expensive back then and Bob didn't feel like paying for them. What he did suggest though was FAKE cameras. Big ones that would almost always dissuade a crook. Nope. Our lawyer nixed it. If we put up fake cameras we are admitting that we know there is a burglary problem in the garage. A problem that we are not addressing properly if the cameras aren't real. That would significantly increase our liability if someone got robbed. To avoid that we were told to not put in those fake cameras even though our customers would have been much better off if we did. Makes a lot of sense doesn't it?

3. Bob decided to stake his daughter Nicole in the final event of the World Series of Poker. A ten thousand dollar investment that was unlikely to be profitable. I don't say that because she was female as there are plenty of excellent female players. But there was another problem. She had never played a hand of any type of poker in her life. And the tournament was in a week. Bob assigned me the task

158

of getting her ready. A favorite saying of my father was "If you give me a difficult assignment, I will do it quickly. If the assignment is impossible it will take me a little longer." I sometimes say the same thing. But I didn't consider "a little longer" to be one week. In any case I had to make the best of it.

I hatched a plan that actually gave her a small chance. In future years it became known as "The System". Move in all your chips or fold. (Tweaked in the special case where she is in the big blind and others only limp in.) The question was which hands to move in with. A move in only strategy actually has a pretty good chance of doing well if it is executed expertly. Which means constantly making adjustments based on a variety of factors. That was too much to expect of Nicole. But even a very simplistic move in strategy is not "drawing dead" as long as there is a decent amount of chips in the pot at the start. I told her to fold everything but a pair of aces or kings the first four hours of the tournament. (late buy ins weren't allowed back then). And after that, if no one had yet entered the pot, move in with any pair, AK, Ax suited, and no gap suited connecters from 54 on up. If someone played in front of her she would revert to needing aces or kings. This strategy would steal most pots and if she was lucky enough to win a few hands when she was called (usually by outdrawing), she would actually accumulate a big stack.

Bob was skeptical that such a simple strategy had even a scintilla of a chance. So he tried it himself. He entered the $1000 buy in tournament the day before the main event. There were about 500 entrants if I remember correctly. He came in fourth! (And if he hadn't deviated from the system on his last hand he might have done better yet. He moved in on the button with AK behind the player on his right who had made a small raise with a pair of tens. It was of course the right play but he was technically disobeying the System's instructions.)

Nicole was not so lucky. She lasted quite a while but eventually ran into a player with a deep stack who was holding two aces.

4. I was taking my beautiful friend Shay to a movie at the Palms Hotel in Vegas. Black father, white mother. A bit younger than me. While we were waiting to buy tickets the subject of physical fitness somehow came up. She had a perfect athlete's body while I didn't. But I actually kept myself in surprisingly good shape having lifted weights most of my life. I told her that I could take a punch in the stomach delivered by her. And she took me up on it right then and there in front of a bunch of people! She hit me hard but I took the punch pretty well as expected. Then this young black kid comes up to me and says "can I do that." Clearly someone who had his eye on Shay and hoped to show off in front of her. Of course, I was annoyed. My bragging about my abs didn't extend past the punching ability of a young female and I was sure he realized that. He was being a jerk. To regain the upper hand, I made an offer to buy the large "bling" around the kid's neck after Shay commented on it. "I'll give you $200 for it" I said to him. He replied "It cost me 750 thousand dollars." "OK sure it did", I replied. "Now please go away." Meanwhile Shay is elbowing me. "Yes, what is it?" "David, that's Floyd Mayweather." Oops.

Chapter 51: The Stratosphere Tower

When Bob and I returned from Russia, we had no lingering doubts about whether to build an observation tower next to the hotel. We really only needed about a million dollars a month to get us back into the black and a tower appeared to be just the ticket to make us at least that much. Not only would we make money off of admissions, shops and restaurants in the tower itself, our casino would undoubtedly benefit as well. And we could raise the price of our Vacation Club packages. So we needed to get to work to make that happen. Get government approval to build it. Find an architect. Find engineers, Find a construction company. And oh, find 50 million dollars.

The second and third tasks were relatively easy. The architect had already designed at least one other tower and the rendering he drew for us was gorgeous. Well over 1000 feet tall with a ten floor pod at the top including both an indoor and outdoor observation deck and, of course, a gourmet revolving restaurant. Getting permission from the county was tougher than we expected. There was supposedly concern that the tower was too close to the airport. The approval of future high-rise construction much closer to airliner's path, pretty much proved that the objectors were just trying to find an excuse to stop Bob's project. But we prevailed in the end.

The 50 million was a different story. We needed either an investor or a scheme to get the money ourselves. Since no investor was forthcoming our only hope was an idea Bob had to form sort of a super Vacation Club similar to time share deals. It worked for a while but then we were stopped by the state of Nevada. Finally, they perceived the possibility of disaster and weren't willing to look the other way. Now what do we do?

At this point we had not even begun construction. And Bob was ready to abandon the whole tower idea before it cost him any serious money. When he mentioned that to me, I asked him two simple questions. "How much cash can you get your hands on?" And after he replied "about ten million" I asked him how far up the tower could be built with that money. He answered that it could be built to the bottom of the pod, about 800 feet. The pod cost the lion's share of the money. Hearing that, I begged Bob to start building. I was sure that we had gotten no investors mainly because they were skeptical of whether the project would actually happen. When they observed that the tower was "halfway" up most of their fears would be allayed. He took my advice and gambled the 10 mil.

And I was right. Although it might have taken a little persuasion from me to close the deal. I had previously gotten Lyle Berman to spend a few tens of thousands of dollars on my first idea (visiting his casinos), and then a few hundred thousand on my second one (marketing my casino poker table games). So how much harder could it be to up the number to about THREE HUNDRED MILLION? Actually, I was only hoping that his company come up with about fifty million. But Lyle was not interested in owning the tower only. Not with a mediocre hotel as its neighbor. He was only interested in the much larger project of a major renovation and expansion of the hotel casino along with the tower. Bob had the opinion that the extra 250 million would not add enough revenue to make it worth spending. He thought there would have been a better return on investment spending only the fifty. There is a decent chance he was right. We will never know. But Bob was not in position to insist. Lyle was willing to bail him out (including buying out or servicing those Vacation Club buyers who had not yet arrived.) He was not about to turn that down. The Stratosphere Tower in Las Vegas is now surely one of the top ten structures in the world and will always stand as a monument to Bob Stupak.

The adjoining hotel is not as iconic and has gone through many owners including multibillionaire Carl Icahn. Bob gave up involvement in the place shortly after the grand opening. I stayed on for a short while and even flew to New York to discuss some ideas with Icahn himself. But y the year 2000 or so I was no longer Resident Wizard and had moved back to southern California for a while to play poker. Bob and I stayed in touch but didn't see each other much. He did enlist me for one last scheme (The Titanic Hotel) but it did not come to fruition. We had one last dinner a few months before he died. A dinner during which he related something to me that, if true, would be front page news even after all these years. That's coming up shortly.

Chapter 52: Two Nice Casino/Sportsbook Ideas of Mine That Interested Icahn

Multi billionaire, corporate raider, Carl Icahn likes to dabble with owning casinos. He also sometimes makes big sports bets. When I met him in Las Vegas I briefly told him about a couple of interesting wrinkles to existing games I had thought up that could be used in a casino or, in one of the cases, a sportsbook. When he got back to New York he invited me to fly out and have dinner with him and discuss them in more detail. He never did put them in his properties as far as I know. But since they were not patented and since the underlying concepts behind them are kind of interesting, I thought I might as well describe them here. Feel free to use them if you happen to own a casino.

Imagine that you are a bookie during football season. Say that you are a legal bookie that usually requires bettors to put up the full amount they could conceivably lose. (But this principle, stated slightly differently, works just as well if you take bets on credit.) A customer comes up to the counter wanting to bet equal amounts on five games. They are routine bets, requiring him to lay 11 to 10 odds. In this case he wants to profit $100 on each winner (against the spread of course. And we will ignore ties for simplicity's sake). So, he gives you $550 for the five $110-$100 bets. But he is frowning and you ask him why. He tells you that he actually likes ten games but since he refuses to bet less than $110 a game and he only has $550 in his pocket, he had to whittle that down to five.

You feign sympathy. And offer him a way to bet the other five games as well. You say you will FORGIVE the debt if he owes more. He can beat you for up to a thousand dollars but the most you can beat him for is 550. And he gobbles up your offer and gives you the name of five more teams he likes.

Do you still have a positive EV doing something like that? Let's do a little math.

The following assumes that each game is a coin flip and that the lines are all half points so they can't end in a tie. But things would normally not change very much even without these assumptions.

When a customer bets 110 to win 100 he is giving you an average of five dollars. (Nowadays the gambling literature often rephrases that to "you have won five Sklansky Bucks" I never promoted that name being fully aware that they are actually "Pascal Bucks.") You will average being ahead ten dollars after two games. Thus, if he bets five such games your EV is $25. And if he were to bet ten such games (normally) it would be $50. So, without enticements, persuading a customer to bet an extra five games makes you an average of an extra twenty-five dollars. But in this case, you are clearly "earning" less than $25 extra because you are not always winning the full amount. If he wins no games at all, your gift to him cost you $550 as he should have lost $1100. If he wins only one game he should have lost $890 rather than $550, so you cost yourself $340. If he goes 2 and 8 you win $130 less than you should. So what does that all mean?

Ironically the relevant figures are exactly the same ones that I used when I made that giant parlay card score. (And in fact if a sportsbook was to implement my idea the most efficient way to do it would probably be with the use of a card that looked like a parlay card.)

If the customer bet ten games on 1024 different occasions (which would normally earn you $51,200) your "generosity" would have cost you:

$550 one time

$340 ten times

$130 forty-five times.

$9800 after 1024 trials. An EV of (negative) 9.57. Instead of earning an average of $50 off of his ten

bets you earn $40.43. But your total win after all those trials is still $41,400.

Meanwhile had you not made this generous offer and restricted him to five bets, you would have

won, on average, only $25,600 after 1024 such scenarios. $25 per scenario.

So, does this mean what it seems to mean? It seems that not only did your "generous offer"

not turn the situation into an unprofitable one for you, it ADDED to you profits. And indeed it did.

$25 dollars turns into $40.43. Plus, you probably received "gratefulness" that you didn't deserve. Yes

you will very rarely have to come up with five hundred extra dollars when he goes 10-0 (or $290 or

$80 for 9-1 or 8-2) But it's a drop in the bucket. Giving him those five extra "free" bets increases

your profit by over 60 percent. (For those who are having trouble believing this, let me remind you

that those extra five bets are also laying 11 to 10. And the final result is for all ten games. So those

extra five bets will, on average, hurt the results of the first five.)

The above "promotion" can be implemented in many ways. It does not have to be "bet ten,

risk no more than five." And it doesn't have to be only for sports bets. It works for even money

paying casino bets as well. But you can't be as generous when the house edge is a lot lower than the

4.5 percent of sports betting. Roulette is fine though (even better would be a roulette video machine).

And if the total number of bets increased, the maximum player loss could decrease. Guarantee a

hundred spins and a hundred equal sized even money bets and you could offer to take no more than

twenty bets when the smoke clears.

My other idea also used roulette. But again, there are myriad variations on a roulette table or

elsewhere, that all use the same mathematical concept. A concept embodied in the famous Birthday

Problem that I'm sure many of you heard of. How many people need to be in a room such that, there is a greater than even chance that there will be at least two who have the exact same birthday? (month and day, not year) Most people are very surprised to hear that the answer is "23." (Some are way off because they misunderstand the question and think a specific person must find a match. That's not true. The match could be the 19th and the 22nd person you survey. But even those who understand the question usually guess much higher than 23.) The math is actually easy (if you assume no one is born on February 29) .Just multiply the probabilities that each succeeding person you ask, after failing to find a match to that point, does not match any previous person surveyed. The chance you would survey 23 people and match none is 364/365 x 363/365 x 362/365 x…...343/365. That comes out to a little bit below one half. Since there is less than a one half chance of getting no match there is a more than one half chance of at least one match.

I extended the principle to a roulette wheel. In America it includes a double zero and has 38 numbers altogether. And if you spin it eight times the chances it will have a number come up twice is over 50 percent. And just like the birthday problem, few would guess that. So that is one reason why allowing a "no repeat in 8 spins" might get good action. But there is a second, perhaps even stronger reason. The buildup of excitement. A buildup experienced by the vast majority of bettors who usually get to five or six spins before they lose. Way more than "halfway" there (oddly analogous to my idea to spend one fifth of the Stratosphere Tower budget to obtain the psychological illusion of getting more than halfway up.)

There are two other ways to bet the "no repeat" besides the even money bet. One way would be to pick a number larger than eight and be paid off at higher odds if you reach that threshold. A casino could easily pay 2-1 for ten, 5-1 for twelve 20-1 for fifteen 400-1 for twenty and 25,000 to 1 for twenty five. And of course, they could offer a progressive jackpot as well. They also might consider using a 37 slat single zero roulette wheel since no repeats are even rarer. 20 spins without a repeat could now pay 500-1 and 25 could pay 50,000 -1! The house edge on regular bets would be approximately cut in half but it might be worth it in return for increasing "no repeat" odds. Another way to bet "no repeat" would be to offer an increasing "free roll" once you have gotten to the gateway number. Perhaps 10 or 11. You might only get even money if you get there and then immediately thereafter repeat. But if you keep going the payoff increases. And then when you do repeat you get the payoff assigned to the streak you had actually reached

Chapter 53: Carl Icahn and Steve Wynn Show Me Their 7th Grade Side

When Carl Icahn decided he would like to hear a bit more about my ideas for casino and sportsbook promotions he offered to fly me out to New York to have dinner with him. We had played poker together a couple of times and Bob Stupak and I had actually visited him at his Las Vegas home. So I wasn't completely shocked when he called me with that invitation. The fact that it was costing him over a thousand bucks just to have dinner with me was flattering but not that not flattering. If he never made another dime his bankroll allowed him to do that every day for the next twenty five thousand years or so. I was actually more flattered that after dinner he walked me all the way back to my hotel, about a half a mile away. Although we had a nice dinner and discussed several interesting subjects we sadly never actually made a financial deal. But don't feel too sorry for him.

During the dinner there were a couple of interesting snippets. After he described a few of his hostile takeovers that made a few hundred million each, I asked him why he still worked so hard at making money when he had far more than he could ever spend. Especially given that, unlike some other billionaires, he was not really building or creating things. I expected an answer along the lines of "I make those corporations more efficient by replacing incompetent management." Not sure

168

whether I was prepared to ask him why he deserves a half a billion for doing that had he answered

that way. But in fact he didn't. Instead he hesitated and thought for a while. Which made it seem like

he had never considered or had been asked that question. Hard as that is to believe. Finally, he

replied "That's just what I do."

Also, during the dinner, out of blue, he blurts out "I have so much fucking money." Weird. It

sounded like something a teenager would say when he passed the ten thousand dollar bankroll mark.

Not something you would expect from the eighteenth or so richest person in the world.

But the Steve Wynn story was even weirder and more juvenile. It began several years after

he bought the downtown Golden Nugget and transformed it into something akin to one of the nicest

strip hotels. At that time Steve sometimes played poker in his cardroom and I think he read my first

book. In any case we were somewhat friendly. And I asked him for a personal favor. There was a

very pretty girl working as a busgirl behind the counter at the Nugget coffee shop who I had my eye

on. One day I asked her why she was not a cocktail waitress given her looks. She replied that she was

only twenty years old. But that she wouldn't be a cocktail waitress even when she was old enough.

Rather she wanted to work with computers once she finished her schooling in the subject. Which

allowed me to mention that I knew the owner of the place and could probably get him to hire her to

work with their computers once she was ready. That, of course, pleased her.

So, the next time I saw Steve I told him about her and asked him if he would walk into his

coffee shop with me for a few minutes and assure her that he would seriously consider her for a

computer job when she completed her training. Especially, of course because his friend David had

told him that she seemed like a very smart girl. He agreed. (And gave heart attacks to the

management of the restaurant who never normally served the big boss who almost always ate at his

gourmet places. Yet here he is walking up to the COUNTER. And engaging the busgirl in a lengthy conversation. I wonder whether they grilled her after we walked out.)

As the years went by, I would engage Steve in conversation only rarely. His eyes were getting progressively worse (retinitis pigmentosa) and he thus didn't stop to chat as he used to, since he usually didn't see me when I was nearby. Plus, he had become a lot busier. And by far the most powerful man in Las Vegas. He had built the amazing Mirage hotel and was about to open the even more amazing Bellagio. And he had stopped playing poker. Then about fifteen or twenty years after doing me that favor, I walk into the Mirage and notice Steve standing in the middle of the pit surrounded by several casino executives where they were immersed in discussion. I walk by not even considering acknowledging him under those circumstances. But then I hear someone calling out "hey David." I turn around and it is Steve motioning me to come to come back to where they were standing in the pit. I immediately assume that they had been discussing some kind of promotion or casino game rule change and when he saw me, he realized that he would like my opinion. That would be great. But I was wrong.

When I reach the group, Steve asks me in front of all the (male) executives. "Do you remember that girl I tried to help you out with back at the Nugget?" "Of course". "Did you ever fuck her."

Chapter 54: Internet Poker Explodes

In the early 2000s I was making five times as much from my books as I was making in the 1990s. As was Mason. Same with our twoplustwo website. And neither of us can claim much credit for that. Rather it was the confluence of three events. Chris Moneymaker won the World Series of Poker championship event. Poker on television could be shown essentially live with the use of the holecard camera. And internet poker was spreading throughout the world. For a while the Amazon top 100 best selling book list included three of mine at the same time! Only JK Rowling and perhaps a few others have ever achieved that. So I sat back, enjoyed my good luck, and cashed my royalty checks.

The website was a different story. A decision had to be made. Do we simply charge for internet poker ads or do we become an "affiliate." As an affiliate we would be paid a percentage of whatever was raked from a player who signed up with an internet poker room via an ad on twoplustwo.com. And we would expect to make several times what we would make if we merely sold ads. The problem was that getting a piece of the rake would have been technically against the law. Because Americans were not allowed to own these poker sites. And profiting in proportion to the rake could be construed as an illegal activity. At least that is what our attorneys told us. So we played it safe. And probably cost ourselves millions. Our competitors chose to gamble and profited accordingly. But that doesn't mean that we made a bad decision. Two reasons. One was that, as by far the biggest entity in the poker world, prosecutors who ignored the smaller entities might have still gone after us. Secondly, we were laying odds. In other words, even if we thought that the chances of going to jail was small that doesn't mean we should take that chance. At least Mason thought that way. Me, I'm not so sure.

Chapter 55: Cliff Notes On My Two "Scandals"

For the most part I'm not bothering to tell you about personal anecdotes that readers might find mildly interesting if I was a celebrity or a very well known person. That's why I say that this isn't an autobiography. But there were two notorious incidents that occurred around this time that I need to briefly summarize so as not to be accused of ignoring things that put me in a bad light.

The bad one involved a very intelligent pretty young girl who, as it turned out, was clearly suffering from some sort of mental illness. Because she eventually (many months after my last contact with her) took her own life. When I met her, she was already making a name for herself by finishing high in some poker tournaments while at the same time being involved in some dramas with other poker players. I thought that I could probably piggyback that notoriety into some publicity for my books. Basically, the idea would be to teach her some advanced concepts, stake her in a few tournaments, and if she did well, she would tout my books and tutoring, plus pay me my end. While this was going on, she apparently decided that she would benefit by telling me that if I was single she would have an interest in me. I didn't really believe that. But since I don't like being "hustled" I decided to subject her to a couple of small "tests" to call her bluff. Which she passed.

She started off great in some small internet tournaments. But then, against my instructions, she blew it all in two big one table tournaments that she knew not how to play. So I ended our deal. At which point she said that she would besmirch me and the woman I was living with unless I continued staking her. I refused with the comment that she could say what she wanted about me but leave out my innocent ladyfriend. She replied that she would be "collateral damage." That didn't go over to well with me and there was some back and forth which I wrote about as it was happening. One of the unfortunate facts about the lady living with me had to do with her mother. And after a pokercast invited the extortionist, they found and printed photos of the mother. The feud with the pretty, smart, lady blew over quickly and she apparently left the poker world. But several months later she killed herself. Not something a healthy person would ever do, in spite of her having alienating many of her friends, considering how easy it would have been for her to turn things around given her very positive attributes. Thus, I assume she had a serious mental illness.

But the owner of the pokercast was not mentally ill. And not only did he print the picture of the mother, he also told me via a messenger that he would take it down for $10,000. In the short run I deemed the best solution was to pay. The mother had been following what was going on and was very upset with her picture being broadcast along with story. Meanwhile a few days previous to the blackmail message, she had told her daughter that her other, younger daughter, had just gotten her driver's license and was desperately was hoping to get a car. Which no one could afford. I called the mother and told her about the blackmailer. I told her I was willing to pay. She told me not to. I told her I would not acquiesce to that desire as I owed it to her. However, I would give her a choice. The 10K would be spent but I would leave it up to her whether it would be used to take the picture down or to buy her daughter a car. She chose the latter.

The other story started about 2002 ago and mostly ended about 2013. To make sure readers don't stop reading in the middle, I will start near the end. A flight to New York around 2011 that I took with a very nice 45 year old lady, who I had known for a while who was willing to help me with a problem, that could use her experience in the medical field. I'll call her Roseanne. My father had died several years earlier and my mother was now living in an apartment in New Jersey getting part time help from a caregiver. It was time to find her a better place. Roseanne and I showed her several assisted living facilities which she eventually rejected in spite of their luxuriousness. Instead she wanted to move to Vegas and be near me. In an apartment. Which is what happened.

When she got here, I quickly needed to hire some sort of "visiting angel" even though at age 87, mom could still pretty much take care of herself. That was problematical because how could I expect someone to be "on call" and show up those times they were needed, but not otherwise? Roseanne had a solution. Hire her and her daughter. They had both recently moved to Las Vegas and if they shared responsibilities, they could pull that off. I agreed and for the next year or so Roseanne and her 27 year old daughter took care of my mother until her death (due to medical malpractice). After that we didn't have too much contact but we remained friendly.

Neither Roseanne or her daughter ever, to my knowledge, expressed any negative feelings about me. Even though ten years previously, Roseanne's daughter ran away from home and moved in with me.

Saura. At least that is what she called herself. Thousands of you already know about her. Many of you have seen her photos that were taken at our two plus two party and posted online (after her return to Vegas.) A lot of you have read her Ask Me Anything Thread written about the same time, on twoplustwo.com. And the reason everybody knows is that I have a pet peeve that I probably take too far. People making fun of "nerds." I feel a responsibility to defend them and make them feel better. Possibly similar to Bill Gates given he said "Be nice to nerds. Because one day you will be working for them." And by outing myself about Saura I took that a step further by maybe giving nerds hope even when it came to beautiful girls. My miscalculation was in not realizing that all aspects of the relationship would be ignored other than the fact that she was only 16 years old.

Of course, I didn't know she was 16. On the chat line where we met, she claimed to be a few days short of 20. And she looked even older. People are skeptical that I didn't know her real age but every one of the dozens of people who met her never had a clue. In fact, she was never carded in the

175

casino, where you have to be 21. She accompanied me in public on numerous occasions. Furthermore, she was smart as a whip and obviously a great liar. My son's first wife, age 30, had some serious conversations with her and even asked for advice on occasion. Of course, even at 20 she was way too young for me but she insisted the age difference didn't bother her. Not being content with that I assigned my son Mat the task of giving her an extensive grilling about that subject to see if he had reservations. He didn't. And neither did my parents who met her on several occasions.

After being together for several months we bought a beautiful house in Vegas and were about to move in. But she left her 7-11 phone in the house which resulted in Roseanne being able to track her down. The details aren't important. A few days later I am awakened by a pounding on the bedroom door. It's the police. They have Saura detained outside and inform me she is 16. What? The cops were not nasty. In fact, the situation was so obvious to them that the lead cop put his arm around me and said "Do not say a word to me. Get a lawyer. They are going to try to sue you for a lot of money." I did. The renowned David Chessnoff, partner to Mayor Oscar Goodman. But the cop was wrong. Not only did Roseanne not sue me, she told Chessnoff that she was totally sympathetic to what happened to me and that Saura had passed for 21 when she was 13.

They brought Saura back to Arizona and incarcerated her in juvenile detention for a few weeks. I assumed I would never see her again. Then I got a call from the Phoenix police. She would be having a hearing soon and they would like me to attend and then bring her back to Vegas! So would her probation officer and so would her mother. They had come to the conclusion, based on what they learned, that it would be best for her. The police would write a letter verifying that. A letter I still have. I wasn't sure how I felt about all that. But I didn't have to decide because the judge put the kibosh on their idea. Saura disappeared for several years, had a neat little boy, and then popped back into my life about ten years later until my mother died. I have talked to her a few times since then and she is doing very well. Which makes me happy.

Chapter 56: Several More General Ideas

Again, some of these have been mentioned over the years in previous writings

1. People almost always underestimate the importance of math/ logic/probability type thinking unless the issue being contemplated is obviously technical. They don't realize, or don't want to realize, that if even a small part of a decision or problem can benefit from those subjects, anyone who doesn't use them is at a disadvantage, everything else being equal, to anyone who does. The most obvious examples occur in sports. Coaches who dismiss probability type analysis when deciding whether to punt, bunt, onside kick or whatever. But these situations occur in many aspects of life. And unsurprisingly, those who push back on this type of analysis are almost always those who didn't know how to do it in the first place. (I realize that I am repeating myself here but the concept is important enough to justify it)

2. One place where the subject of probability needs to be invoked is "me too" accusations of sexual assault by people they know. The problem is that the normal standard of "acquit unless guilty beyond a reasonable doubt" is too vague. Because an acquittal or even a prosecutor's reluctance to prosecute, results in a stigma toward the accuser. Occasionally an accuser is pretty obviously lying perhaps due to psychological reasons. But most of the time there is something there even if it can't be proven. Just as in those crimes where I recommend a "probably guilty" verdict when it is appropriate, for serious crimes, something similar should probably be used to avoid stigma to accusers who can't completely prove their case.

3.One of the coolest presents you can give someone is a surprise visit from a good friend or close relative who, because of physical distance, they haven't seen in a long time. Fly them in, hide them in a closet, and tell the person their birthday or whatever gift is in that closet. I have done that three times in my life and it worked great each time.

4.In rare cases you may have the opportunity to do kind of the opposite to the above to someone who has wronged you. Totally legal revenge. The idea is to take advantage of the psychological fact that someone's emotions depend more on something surprisingly good or surprisingly bad happening rather than simply the situation they are in. Thus, if someone has been taking advantage of you but doesn't realize that you are on to them, one way to get back at them would be make them expect something terrific and then have it not happen. You are probably too nice to do something like that but I did it once and it made me feel better. (The details are described in DUCY.)

5. There are two different kinds of probabilities in the real world and it might be useful to you to understand the difference. I call them baseball vs boxing probabilities although there are much fancier words for them. When you are betting on a baseball game and team A is deemed 60 percent to beat team B it is usually somewhat different than if you are betting a boxing match and boxer A is deemed 60 percent to beat boxer B. Do you see why? In the first case there is very little doubt that baseball team A is the better team. Team B will win 40 percent of the time because an individual baseball game involves a lot of luck and often luck will cause the slightly less skillful team to emerge victorious. But in the boxing case the 60 percent probability typically comes from our uncertainty as to which boxer is actually better. Technically one could say that both probabilities stem from lack of knowledge. In one case it's our ignorance of their skill while in the other case it is our ignorance of

how the ball will bounce. But that's a dumb take and I only mention it so as not to be criticized by hi falutin mathematicians. Here is another way to look at it. How would you alter your assessment if they played both contests twice and the underdog won the first game in both cases? Hopefully you realize that in the baseball case the favorite would usually barely move down, perhaps to 59 percent (it would depend mainly on how confident you are in your original 60 percent assessment and perhaps on how lopsided the score was.) But in the boxing case, the underdog winning would almost always make him the favorite in the second fight, again depending on how clearly he won the first fight. The added information of the first boxing match is worth a lot more than the first baseball game.

6. The saying "first do no harm" that doctors supposedly follow is, of course, flawed. If Robin always followed that edict when she was a paramedic, people who are alive today wouldn't be. If the EV of a drug or medical procedure is higher than the EV of doing nothing then you should probably do it. Ironically though it is almost certain that in real life many doctors err not because they follow the edict but rather because they don't. Doing nothing, even when it has the higher EV is something people in many fields resist whether they be doctor's, lawmaker's or whatever, especially if they are not completely secure in their jobs and are afraid that no action will be looked down upon.

7. When someone is accused of major wrongdoing it is a little unfair to assume he is guilty when he doesn't defend himself and refers questions to his lawyer. Because in many cases he is in fact guilty of minor wrongdoing and he can't explain why he is innocent of the major charge without admitting his guilt to the minor one. Perhaps you are not sympathetic to his plight because the people you know commit neither major nor minor crimes. But that's not the case for me.

8. As I write this, America is in the midst of uncompromising opinions on a myriad of matters. Depending on who you are listening to you will hear that x is either unquestionably right or unquestionably wrong. You don't know enough about the issue to have an opinion so you are hoping to rely on others. But how can you do that when others strongly disagree? As I originally pointed out in DUCY there are five factors. The first four are of approximately of equal importance. If two people are expressing opposite viewpoints about a subject about which you are ignorant, the opinion you should lean towards depends on how knowledgeable they are about the subject, how smart they are in general, how strongly they feel they are right, and whether they personally gain by persuading others to agree with them. On occasion though there is a fifth factor. Do one of the two debaters pride themselves on virtually always being right to the point that they won't even enter the debate unless they are absolutely sure they are correct? If they are sane and reasonably intelligent you can probably throw the other factors out the window and bet on them.

Chapter 57: Experiencing A Home Invasion

It was sometime around 2007. I was living in a small group of nice houses southeast of the Mandalay Bay. There was a gate but no guard. I had a dispute with my alarm company and temporarily had no alarm at all. I wasn't worried about it since all the neighbors knew each other and would quickly recognize anything suspicious. I sometimes even carelessly left the front door unlocked. Bad idea, especially since it was World Series of Poker time and I figured to have a bunch of money on me.

I'm sleeping in my bedroom at about 3AM after coming back from the RIO a couple of hours earlier. All of a sudden, my door flies open and there is a guy standing in the doorway with a scarf around his face and a gun in his hand. He says "Don't look at me." Thank goodness. Surely you see why. I told him that I had no intention of looking at him and that this would be the easiest robbery he ever did. He brought me into another room, had me lay down on the couch, and after having me empty my pockets, he and his partner walked through the house in search of valuables. They didn't find much jewelry but they did find a $5000 chip. Apparently, they hadn't chosen me because of poker because the guy walks back into the room and asks me what I did for a living. I realized later that it was probably because of the chip. When I told him I was a professional poker player he got a bit excited and said something like "Really? Do you need a bodyguard?" I swear. In other words, every time someone points a gun at my head, they ask me to be their friend five minutes later. First Joe, then Robin, and now an apparently unemployed home invader. Don't ask me why. Meanwhile something weird immediately pops into my strange brain. I start thinking about those unhappy housewives who try to get rid of their husbands by finding some seedy guy from their neighborhood who perhaps just got out of jail and offering them ten thousand dollars to have hubby killed. They

182

don't realize that invariably the bad guy will pretend to play along while secretly going to the cops. Then he will wear a wire and she is arrested the day she hands over money. Ex criminals are far more likely to try to earn brownie points by snitching on a "straight" person who is trying to recruit them rather than actually going along with the plot, so such recruitment techniques will almost always backfire. The only exception would be if the bad guy you were trying to recruit couldn't possibly consider snitching because he was still committing major crimes and would want nothing to do with the police. Like my home invader. Would that have been the first thing you thought of?

During the robbery the guy made a phone call. I later realized that he was probably talking to someone in a car outside the gate. I also belatedly realized that living in a small gated community with no guards on patrol may actually increase the chances of getting robbed. Because with only one way in, a lookout can see whether cops are on the way from a pretty large distance. I wouldn't be surprised if people living in normal houses on normal streets are actually safer.

Before leaving, my job seeker asked me if I minded if he takes my car out for a spin. He assured me that it would be discovered within the hour. It was. When the police brought me to it, I quickly inspected the car for any problems. There weren't any. Furthermore, the dozen or so copies of my poker books on the back seat were still there. Evidently even armed home invaders have a line they won't cross.

Chapter 58: My Best Idea

Strangely the idea that I call my "best" has almost certainly been thought of by thousands of others before me. It is a lot more obvious than most of my other ideas. I believe the reasons it has not been implemented previously is because there are a few arguments against it that seem persuasive. But they are not. And I will explain why shortly. Meanwhile I give it my "best" rating for two reasons. It will sometimes right a serious wrong. And it could be implemented almost instantly.

Put simply I propose that in "closed" cases where people are serving long terms in prison for crimes that are no longer being actively investigated, someone who actually did the crime, be given amnesty if he confesses in order to free the innocent, unjustly, incarcerated inmate.

The case has to be closed. The innocent inmate has to be facing years more in jail. The "confessor" has to subject himself to investigation and the threat of being charged with a felony if it can be proved he was lying.

Now let's deal with the objections.

1.   There are very very few innocent people serving long sentences in jail.

Recent exonerations based on DNA evidence has shown that not to be true. There are hundreds of such cases. Hundreds out of millions are not much except from those you can extrapolate to many thousands. Because only a small percentage of old crimes are of a nature where DNA could exonerate. Plus, there is the unfortunate fact that in our past, many juries were willing to convict minorities while they still harbored "reasonable doubt".

2. The actual perpetrator will almost never come forward even if he knows he won't be prosecuted for the crime.

I'm not so sure. I think some people, even criminals or ex criminals, feel enough guilt about their part in having an innocent person rot in jail that they would avail themselves of the program in spite of the stigma they bring on themselves. Others would do it simply to relieve themselves of the worry hanging over their heads that somehow their guilt would eventually be discovered. And of course you could even include a small reward to nudge even more guilty to confess. In any case why does it even matter if the percentage of guilty people take advantage of my suggested program is small? Some will. And that is better than none.

3. It would be disgusting to officially give amnesty to a person who committed a terrible crime.

So what? Because we consider it much worse to convict an innocent person than to acquit a guilty one, we essentially already give "amnesty" to thousands of serious criminals every year when we acquit them due to reasonable doubt. The disgustingness of giving amnesty to the confessor pales in comparison to the disgustingness of allowing innocents to remain imprisoned.

4. Clever people can scam this program, even perhaps, via a plan before the crime is committed.

First of all, I seriously doubt that such a scam would be attempted very often. Remember that I suggest jailtime for perjured confessions. And I'm pretty sure that almost all fraudulent confessions by innocent people, even the ones who think they have studied the crime well, have holes in them.

But more importantly we have to get back to the concept that jailing an innocent person is a much bigger sin than freeing a guilty one. The magnitude of that sin does not change just because the person is sitting in a jail cell rather than being put through a trial. The small possibility of a successful scam should not be a consideration.

Chapter 59: Some Free Ideas For Casinos and Internet Sites

1. Restructure your rebate system for Baccarat hi rollers. Make it more like catastrophe insurance. In other words, don't give them a small flat rebate like 15 percent on everything they lose but rather something like 50 percent on everything they lose above a certain fairly large amount. This will cost less than the other rebate plan yet will probably please customers more.

2. Expose a few cards before the poker deal which will be out of play. This will deter bots as well as force players to think on the fly rather than just memorize strategy algorithms

3. On triple play poker machines that pay big jackpots for three Royals all at once, add a jackpot for two Royals which is actually harder to obtain.

4. After 80 percent of a poker tournament field is gone, have the computer distribute half of the total prize money into the accounts of the remaining players in proportion to their chip counts. Doing that reduces the ultra tight "survival" play that is sometimes the theoretically proper strategy in certain stages of the tournament and instead rewards normal expert play.

5. Hi Lo Split Stud where the high hand gets 60 percent of the pot. Either Eight or Better or Regular. This allows more high type starting hands to be played and also makes the game more interesting.

6.   Offer a poker machine that keeps track of your last hundred hands and pays a nice jackpot if you have made flushes in all four suits during those hands. This builds up excitement, entices players to stay longer, and sometimes changes correct strategy.

7.   Two rounds of betting on each round. Or perhaps on the river only.

8.   Disallow pocket aces or kings in holdem. Except as a bluff. If there is a showdown they can't win (other than to tie each other.) That makes looser starting hand play more justifiable.

9.   Pay big bonuses on keno tickets if winning numbers were chosen in the first ten.

10. Poker machines that offer settlements before the draw. Those settlements need not always be a bad deal or always the same every time for a particular hand.

I have lots more if anyone is interested.

Chapter 60: Some Outside the Box Probability Ingenuity

Earlier I mentioned how so-called experts in sports betting or stock picking usually fail miserably when they publicize their picks ahead of time. So why are they considered experts? It's because they know the general subject well. Batting averages, price earnings ratios, yards gained per rush, balance sheets, or whatever. The problem is that doesn't mean they are smart. Just knowledgeable. In the movie Amadeus the "mediocre" (by world class standards) composer Salieri is shown in a famous scene sneaking a peek at music that Mozart was working on. He is enchanted with it and can be seen swaying with delight. But he is not actually hearing anything. Rather he is just looking at notes on paper. He had become so familiar with musical symbols that his brain had learned to instantly translate them into "sound" in his mind. But this talent, in the movie at least, wasn't enough to put him in in the highest category of his profession.

I contend that it is somewhat the same regarding math. Good but not great mathematicians appear smarter than they are because they can instantly turn mathematical symbols into a thought. Just like you don't have to sound out letters to read a word familiar to you. They rely to a large degree on things they have learned rather than figured out themselves. Here are three examples from the field of probability.

1. I flip a coin and win instantly if it comes up heads. If its tails, you flip and win with a head. If not, it goes back to me and we continue to flip alternately until one of us finally gets a head. Since I go first, I'm obviously the favorite. But what exactly are my chances? Most people who know math add up my chances for winning on each round. $1/2 + (1/2 \times 1/2 \times 1/2) + (1/2 \times 1/2 \times 1/2 \times 1/2 \times 1/2)$ ….etc corresponding to my chances of winning on the first, or third, or

fifth …...flip. It's an infinite sum that adds up to two thirds. But there is a simpler, more

clever way that does not require you to know how to find the sum of a "geometric

progression". Just notice that regardless of which "inning" results in a winner the first flipper

has twice the chances of the second. One half vs one fourth. (Because the second guy needs

both a tail from you and a head from him,) No matter when the game ends the first player's

chances are double the second player. Two thirds.

2.   I have two dollars and you have one dollar. We flip coins for a dollar per flip until one of us

is broke. What are my chances of winning the "freezeout"? If we call my chances z then after

the first flip your chances will either be zero (and mine are 1) or, if you won, it will be you

whose chances become z, (while mine are 1-z.) Thus if the coin is fair my chances (z) are

(1/2 x1) +[1/2 x (1-z)]. Thus z = 1/2 +1/2 -z/2. 3z/2 =1. 3z=2. z=2/3. I will win two out of

three freezeouts. That was pretty simple algebra wasn't it? But it was completely

unnecessary. The solution is instantaneous if you use the simple logical technique of realizing

that if you are playing many such fair contests, the ultimate result must be to break even. And

in order for us to break even in the long run I must win two out of three.

3.   A certain country requires the billion (fertile) married couples in their country to have as

many children as necessary in order have exactly one boy. Assuming that boys are born half

of the time (and there is somehow no limit to how many children a couple will have while

trying for a boy [and no one has multiple births]) how many children will be born? The

slavish math person will notice that 500,000,000 will have one child (boy), 250,000,000 will

have two (girl, boy), 125,000,000 will have three (girl, girl boy), 62,500,000 will have four (girl, girl, girl, boy,) 31,250,000 will have five (girl, girl, girl, girl, girl boy) etc. etc. and he will add up that infinite series. If he knows how. In mathspeak one multiplies a billion by the sum of the series [(n/(2 to the nth power)]. 1/2, 2/4, 3/8, 4/16, 5/32 etc. The answer happens to be "2". Which means that the answer to the question is that two billion children will be born. Unlike the first two questions ninth grade math doesn't cover the technique that the math person might use to get the solution. It's more like college math.

On the other hand, if you want to think a bit, you can use first grade math. And remember that when everybody finishes doing their duty, there will be a billion boys born. Which means there will be a billion girls born. Two billion total

(Note: you can also think in the other direction and come up with the sum of various series by finding a logic problem like this that corelates with it.)

Chapter 61: Bob's Stupak's Astonishing "Revelation"

It was sometime early in 2009. I hadn't talked to Bob, who was struggling with his health, in quite a while. He was in and out of the hospital and sadly died later that year. When I saw him at the Bellagio I told him that I was in the midst of writing a book where he was prominently mentioned (DUCY) and I wanted to tell him about it. He invited me to have dinner with him downstairs at Prime.

We talked about many different subjects that would be covered in the book. It was a very friendly conversation. Mainly about our schemes and our adventures together. One of those adventures was, of course, the 1987 Las Vegas mayor's race where he lost to Ron Lurie in the runoff election after getting by far the most votes in the primary (but not 50 percent which would have been an instant win.) Some people were suspicious of that second election, including the Las Vegas Bullet (owned by Bob) that ran some stories detailing their suspicions. Personally, I never paid attention to those conspiracy theories even though I knew that the powers that be were horrified at the idea that Bob might win. (They were wrong to be because I had resolved to make sure that he would actually do a good job if he won. But few knew that.) After all, fixing an election is a really big crime even for a dopey race for a mayor with little power.

But the election was not one of the things we reminisced about in any detail. It only really came up as an off the cuff comment that Bob made to me out of the blue. I will quote what I believe are close to his exact words.

"Oh, by the way, it turns out that I actually did win that election. They did fix the results. I recently had lunch with Ron Lurie (who is still alive as of this writing) and he admitted it to me. He told me the Mormon Church was behind it."

Chapter 62: What's Next

The last several years haven't been all that interesting. At least not interesting enough to write about. Money stopped growing on trees partially because internet poker became illegal in America and partially because people started to realize that professional players rarely lost to amateurs. At least when playing no limit holdem, which had become by far the most popular game. So I've concentrated instead in getting in good shape. Which for those of you over 50, mainly means a low pulse rate. Mine is about 54. I also had a little fun debating people on our politics forum (twoplustwo.com) for a while. Until it became obvious that my opponents were not interested in following a logical argument wherever it took them, unless it took them where they wanted to go. And I added a few books to my repertoire. Including The Theory of Poker Applied to No Limit, which has gotten very good reviews.

With this book my main goal was to consolidate a lot of ideas I have had over the years that I think are important. Many of them I've put in print elsewhere but I wanted them all in the same place to increase the chance they are read. Plus, there are many ideas I have never written about before. The entertaining and juicy gossipy stuff in the book I consider secondary and view mainly as a way to help sell a book that contains the ideas I mentioned. Sort of like how Steve Wynn built casinos to help him finance the beautiful hotels he loved to erect or how John De Lorean dealt cocaine to finance the crafting of his unique automobiles.

Obviously, playing poker and other types of gambling for a living is not a great way to contribute to society. Writing about poker is possibly slightly more admirable. But only if the emphasis is on how to think about the game rather than simply giving tactics tips. So my dad wouldn't be too proud of those two aspects of my life. This book and a few others of mine are more akin to what he would admire. That is important to me, especially as he didn't get a chance to reach his potential, (though thousands did benefit from his knowledge.) Essentially as far as I am concerned, he was the human equivalent of Graustark.

But there is still one more task that lays ahead for me (not including math tutoring and casino consulting which I plan to get back into. Plus continuing to push for poker/Alzheimer's research and diversifying poker games.). One that would have pleased him mightily. A book about Algebra for those who struggle with it. One unlike any Algebra Made Easy kind of book yet written. It will be way different and, I think, way better. Tentative title: Algebra For Ten Year Olds (And Maybe You).

Plans after that might involve around something I wrote over twenty years ago. The last chapter of Poker Gaming and Life. Which I now reprint.

An Unexpected Ending

Pretend that you are living in the 23rd century. Now I would like you to consider the following hypothetical scenario. You have some kind of horrible accident that leaves you completely paralyzed. Medical science has still not found a way to cure this. You have no close friends or family that you can expect to visit you in the hospital. Things look bleak. You have no desire to spend your days in a wheelchair that you control with your eyelids. However, there is an alternative. It involves going to a special hospital built just for cases like yours. This is what you choose.

When you first arrive at the hospital you are put into a room that has a TV directly over the bed facing down at you. You are aware of your surroundings, but your attention is mainly on the TV. After all, you can't get much enjoyment from the real world. In a few days the hospital staff shuts out the real world completely. They do this by fitting to your head something similar to goggles. The TV show is broadcast to the inside of each lens. (Such things exist even now.) Since you are totally paralyzed, you are now completely unaware of anything except what you see and hear on TV. Doctors are still attending to you and you are being fed intravenously, but you can't tell.

Once the hospital staff has seen that you have adjusted to the goggles and your new state of affairs, they take you to the next step. That is, they disconnect your goggles from the commercial TV station, and instead, connect it to a closed circuit TV camera and microphone. But this TV camera is mounted on a robot that can move around. Furthermore, what makes the robot move are your brain waves! (Please understand that this is not at all farfetched. Brain activity is simply electricity, and even today we have some simple devices that can be made to move or work by a person's thoughts when his brain waves are suitably connected to the device.)

So we have this robot that can move around, following your thought commands (just as your real body once did) and the hospital staff puts it out in the real world, preferably your hometown. Lo and behold, you can once again see and hear things outside your hospital bed. When people encounter your robot on the street, they will know that if they speak to it or show it something, they are really speaking and dealing with you (or at least some person in a hospital bed). So you can see people, enjoy a sunset, or even watch TV by planting your robot in front of a set.

Now as years go by, various technical improvements are made to your robot. The first one is the addition of a voice synthesizer that is connected to the language center of your brain. It's done in such a way that when you think of words the robot speaks them. (We are now beyond our present technology, but I don't think by much.) Now you can really interact with people from the outside world since you can talk to them! And when your robot happens to come upon another comparably equipped robot, your robot can have a conversation with it. Of course, we know that it is really one paralyzed person talking to another paralyzed person.

The next step is to make the robots more human looking and to add the other three senses; taste, touch, and smell. Now you can live an almost normal life. Though you are lying in bed, you are barely aware of it. You live life through your robot. If you have your robot eat food, *you* taste it. If you have your robot patronize a massage parlor *you* feel it. If there are male and female robots, you can even make love. The bottom line is that your robot can become a regular member of the community even though everybody knows that it is really you and your thoughts and desires that they are dealing with when they are interacting with your robot.

At this point it becomes not at all uncommon to see a robot walking down the street. After all, the technology is so wonderful that it is offered to all paralyzed people. But a problem arises. Though robots look fairly similar to human beings, they are different and this makes some people

197

uncomfortable. So a proposal is made that since there are so many of these robots around, why not just set aside a special place for them only. Let them interact with each other. And the proposal is enacted.

All of the robots, including yours, are shipped off to another place — maybe an island, maybe another planet, maybe even another dimension. Still it's not so bad. Your only companions are now other robots, but *they* are connected to real people just as yours is. And you can do basically the same things you could do before your accident and enjoy these things almost as much; this is especially true if you can forget about the fact that you are really lying in a hospital bed, as are all your new found friends (and lovers?). Which is why a few years later, on one particular night, a group of human do gooders sneak into all of the hospital rooms around the world that contain paralyzed people attached to robots. They then proceed to give all these patients, including you, an injection. This injection puts you to sleep for a while after which you wake up with a permanent case of full fledged amnesia!

So what do you think when you wake up? That is a tough question. But one thing is for sure; you don't know that you are really lying in a hospital bed. When your robot touches its face, you feel it, but you have no idea that "you" aren't right there in robot land. There is no way for you to tell that the seat of your consciousness is thousands or millions of miles away, or in another dimension. The same goes for all the other robots. If you think about it, you will understand that there really is no way to tell that "you" are not your robot. But I take that back because there *is* one way to tell. Suppose one day after this mass amnesia inducing incident, another robot chases your robot with an axe. You try to get away, but you fail. As the axe comes arcing towards your robot's "head," you say to yourself "I am about to die." When the axe finds its mark, everything goes black; no sights, no sounds, no smells, or anything else. After all, your destroyed robot was your only link to the outside

198

world. But there is something strange. You can still *think*. Somehow you are not really dead. And of course you are not. But notice that there was no way that you could realize this until the robot, that you thought was "you" no longer existed as a viable entity. Your robot had to "die" before you could understand how you live on.

Now wouldn't it be nice if your body was merely a robot like the one in this story, rather than being the real you? But wait a second. How do you know that it's not?